Adventure on Ararat

by
John D. Morris

INSTITUTE FOR CREATION RESEARCH
2716 Madison Avenue
San Diego, California 92116

Cover Photo
Greater and Lesser Ararat

Library of Congress Number 73-79062

TABLE OF CONTENTS

Foreword

When Noah's ark is finally discovered, it will undoubtedly prove to be the greatest archeological find of all time. For years this possibility was so remote it was hardly considered worthy of newspaper space. But all that has changed!

Fernand Navarra's hand-tooled wood, brought to Paris from Mt. Ararat, along with many other reports and rumors, has sparked a new interest in climbing that ancient mountain, referred to in the Bible as the final resting place for the ark. Today there are at least two books, as well as many articles that have been written on the subject, most of them based in large part on Eryl Cummings' twenty-six years of research on stories of sightings of Noah's old craft.

A great many red-blooded Christian young men have dreamed of finding Noah's ark and would leap at an opportunity to go on such an expedition. John Morris, a Los Angeles engineer, did just that. He organized a team of five men, under the direction of the Institute for Creation Research in San Diego, to climb Mt. Ararat in search of the ark in 1972. He was asked to keep a diary of each day's events. Fortunately for you, he did, for now the thousands of us who would love to make such a trip, but never will, are able to get a glimpse of that awesome mountain through his eyes.

Even though he did not locate the ark this trip, John Morris has a story to tell that will excite even the most phlegmatic reader. This diary will be well worth your time, but I warn you, it will increase your desire to go in search of the great ship yourself!

This diary is factual. It reveals the human weaknesses of the five climbers and shows the many unexpected trials of the search, but it also has a gripping message that fires the imagination and stirs one's spirit of adventure. It also reaffirms a conviction I've had for a long time — no one will make this great discovery without God's supernatural help.

1972 was not the year of discovery, but one of these years soon might be! John and his crew have eliminated a large area on the mountain from further consideration and are making plans to concentrate on another very promising area. After reading this account, you may wonder why he wants to try a second search. Like others before him, it's now in his blood — it's a quest. Some day it will be found, Lord willing, and when it is, it will be by men with the dedication of John Morris.

Tim F. LaHaye, D.D.
San Diego, California

Are You Sure You Want to Look for the Ark???

Dear —————————:

Thank you for your letter indicating your interest in joining our Ararat expedition. We are still in need of men to join us in the search, but have made it a matter of real prayer that the Lord make known His will to us and that the right group of men will be drawn together.

Before any decision is made concerning your personal involvement, I would like to acquaint you with our specific plans and also the dangers involved. If, after reading this letter and seeking God's will, you still feel led to join us, contact me or my second-in-command, John Seiter, at this same address.

To begin with, each member of the team will be required to undergo a week of intensive training on Mt. Hood, near Portland, Oregon, to master the techniques of glacial travel, rescue, and survival. This training is scheduled for the middle of June.

While I have no doubt that you are physically fit and can successfully climb Mt. Ararat, I want to make sure that you realize the dangers and hardships involved. For the most part, we will be on or just below a glacier, the permanent icecap of the mountain. Problems with crevasses, landslides, rockslides, and blizzards will be everyday occurrences. When not on the glacier itself, we will be traveling through and sleeping in the territory of the Kurds. The Kurds live on the slopes of the mountain and are subject to no formal legal system. Some of them are also capable of slitting one's throat as he sleeps. The Turkish Army, which patrols the area, will not allow us to continue the search if we are suspected of any anti-Turkish activities, since Mr. Ararat is near the border of Turkey and Russia. Some people have been shot instantly in such situations, and others arrested for spying.

My point is this — this endeavor should not be confused with a romantic adventure. There is a real possibility of injury and even death. In fact, the obstacles are so numerous that a successful search would be impossible without the help of God.

Concerning finances, each member of the team is responsible for paying his own way. No general appeal for money has been made, simply because we want to remain inconspicuous. Several people have donated money throughout the past few months and it will be used for needs that concern the entire group. The personal cost for each person will be $2000.

Dedication to the task of finding the Ark is a prime requirement and is an overriding issue in the selection of personnel. Of

Mt. Ararat from plain.

VIII

the five man team, only three will be together on the upper reaches of the mountain at any time. These three, however, will have to climb the treacherous slopes with up to a 75-pound pack on their backs, endure extreme weather conditions, eat lukewarm dehydrated food, and sleep in a crawl-in tent for a week at a time. Each member must be willing to take orders and submit to the leader's direction. There will be no room for arguments, bickering, and insubordination.

Upon returning to the states, it is hoped that we will have the chance to share our experiences with interested churches and schools. Our purpose in searching for the Ark is not to gain wealth or fame but to win souls for Jesus Christ, and our hope is that the evidence we bring back will cause many people to believe God's Word. It is likely that many churches and Christian groups will desire speakers who were directly involved with the discovery of the Ark to come and share their experiences and findings with them. We have an obligation to God to use this opportunity to further His kingdom here on earth. If this is not your goal and desire as a Christian, then you should not consider joining our group.

Let me summarize the requirements for prospective personnel in order of their importance, as I see them:

1. Theology—Be sound in conservative Christian doctrine and have a deep desire to see people come to know Jesus Christ as their Lord and Saviour.
2. Dedication—Have a willingness to risk life and health to find Noah's Ark because of its evangelical implications.
3. Personality—Have a personality that is harmonious with the others in the group and a determination to maintain goodwill and peace.
4. Speaking Ability—Possess the means and desire to tell others of the meaning of Noah's Ark.
5. Physical Ability—Have the physical strength and endurance needed to climb one of the highest mountains in the world.
6. Financial Backing—The ability to pay one's own way or to raise the support without any commitments to non-Christian organizations.

I have tried to portray to you in this letter just what to expect in regard to our trip. I have been as honest and straightforward as possible. I want to make sure that you know what is involved before you reaffirm your desire to join our group. I think you should talk it over with your family and diligently seek God's will before making a decision.

Please write me and tell me more about yourself, your religious background and Christian life, your personal dedication to this cause, and your thoughts about the trip. We have prayed daily that the Lord will provide the right men for the job, and if He has spoken to you in this matter, please let me know.

Yours for the Ark,

John D. Morris

———

In the months preceding the Institute for Creation Research's expedition to Mt. Ararat, many qualified and concerned individuals contacted me and asked to be included in the search. Each applicant was made a real matter of prayer and frequently I wrote a short letter or made a telephone call to inform these men that the Lord did not seem to indicate that they were the right ones for the job. But there were three men, to whom I wrote the preceding letter. These three men had the right qualifications and the more we prayed about them the clearer it became that these were the men whom God had chosen to continue the search for the remains of Noah's Ark.

Chapter One
Because It's There

For the past twenty-five years, many dedicated men have followed the trail of Noah's Ark. Many of these men are my personal friends. Two of these men, Eryl Cummings and Clifford Burdick, encouraged me to join the search.

Cummings, a born adventurer and explorer, has compiled a large research file on the existence of the Ark and has directed numerous expeditions to Mt. Ararat. Burdick, a geologist, has accompanied Cummings on most of the expeditions and has determined the geologic structure and history of the area.

July 1971

While Eryl Cummings attempted to obtain official permission, Dr. Burdick, Mike Turnage (a biology teacher from Houston), and I prepared to fly to Turkey, join Cummings, and assist him in the search for the Ark. A mere two weeks from departure date, however, Cummings called and advised us not to come, that the anticipated permits had not been granted.

The situation looked bleak — so bleak, in fact, that it seemed that permits would never again be given to an expedition to search Mt. Ararat. It took a couple of days to recover from the shock, but slowly a new plan began to emerge. Perhaps we could

1

launch another expedition in the summer of 1972, with completely new personnel and a completely new mode of operation. We could capitalize on the previous expeditions by changing the usual approach to Turkey, an approach to which the other, well-known expeditions were firmly committed. We could go into Turkey as tourists, carrying only mountain climbing and photographic equipment, apply for permits as tourists to climb the mountain, and if God allowed, to locate the Ark. We would leave behind the sophisticated ice crushing, drilling, sonar, and infra-red equipment and, as inconspicuously as possible, search for any promising remains. We felt that the Ark must first be definitely located, then professional, well-financed expeditions could document the findings.

October 1971

Dr. Burdick and I visited Ararat together. Burdick was the lecturer of a tour of the Middle East (partially sponsored by the Bible-Science Association of Caldwell, Idaho) to study particularly the archeology and geology of Turkey, Lebanon, Israel, and Egypt. I was one of the tour members.

We spent three days at the base of Mt. Ararat. Dr. Burdick and I talked almost continually, day and night. Since he recognized that he probably would never revisit Ararat, at least to continue the search for the Ark, he gladly passed along any information that might be helpful in my search.

Together we studied the geological formations. He showed me many evidences of a worldwide flood and explained how to recognize and interpret them. We visited an ancient cave with carvings on the walls indicating pre-Hittite origins. A heavy snowfall prohibited us from driving to the Russian side of the mountain and seeing the Ahora Gorge.

February 1972

I enrolled in an intensified course in the Turkish language with a private teacher, designed to give me a working knowledge of conversational and colloquial Turkish. Plans were in high gear. Mike Turnage, from Texas, was buying the equipment necessary for our expedition. He recommended that a friend of his also be

Greater Ararat and surrounding marshes.

Lesser Ararat and surrounding marshes.

included in the expedition, but since we intended to take five men, we continued to look for additional personnel. Spirits were high as we made preparations because it was obvious that the Lord Himself was guiding and opening doors.

Through Christian friends living in Turkey, we were assured of the availability of a Land Rover, already in Turkey, a contact man to whom we could ship supplies, and a Kurdish man who had lived near Ararat until converted to Christianity, who would be willing to join our search.

March 1972

DISASTER! Disaster from all directions struck the plans for the expedition as swiftly and suddenly as an Israeli air raid on Egypt.

F:rst, my partner, Mike Turnage, became deathly ill and was forced into a long convalescence period.

Second, his friend decided not to participate since Mike could not.

Third, word came from Turkey that the Land Rover was not available.

Fourth, the newly formed Institute for Creation Research, our sponsoring organization, was experiencing severe financial difficulties.

Fifth, more word from Turkey indicated that the Kurdish Christian had been drafted by the Turkish Army and was unable to join us.

Sixth, I too became sick. I had been studying long hours, trying to learn Turkish, archeology, history of Ararat, etc., in my spare time, and I had discarded normal health procedures. I was subject to severe chest pains and fainting.

It seemed that the whole thing had collapsed. No one was left except me, and I was in no condition to carry on; but throughout it all, even when there seemed to be no hope, I felt the Lord leading, guiding, and urging me to continue the preparations.

April 1, 1972

Since I was trying to save as much money as possible for the

4

intended trip to Ararat, I asked a friend of mine from church, John Seiter, to move in and share my apartment.

John, a very dedicated Christian, planned to marry at the end of May and also needed to save his money.

April 3

John and his fiancée had the last in a long series of arguments, and, with more time on his hands, he began to take deep interest in my work.

April 14

After weeks of prayer, John finally decided that the Lord was also leading him to Mt. Ararat.

John was not a mountaineer (for that matter, neither was I), but he had backpacking experience. John is a deliberate man, and his habit of studying a situation for a long time before acting was a steadying influence on me and several times saved me from making costly mistakes, for I am prone to tackle a problem and try to solve it as soon as I see a need. John was 28 years old and a very likable fellow.

April 16

I flew to Washington, D.C. to attend a board meeting of Search, Inc., a well-financed group of men also dedicated to the discovery of Noah's Ark. They also intended to try to obtain permission to place a large group of well-equipped scientists on Ararat in the summer. I made known my plans to lead a small group of men in hopes that one of our methods would succeed, and all in attendance thought it was a good idea. Mr. Cummings was also present; we talked for hours.

When the meeting was over, John Bultema, an industrialist from Michigan, expressed a desire to affiliate with the ICR expedition. He felt that he could better contribute to the success of our small group than to the larger and more complicated search. He asked to be included in the team that would investigate the mountain. We both agreed to pray about it before making any decisions.

April 24

Roger Losier, a 23-year-old graduate of Dallas Bible College, wrote a letter to me and asked to join the expedition. His letter indicated a real desire to serve the Lord in this project and a willingness to sacrifice and work hard to bring it to a successful conclusion. A few letters and phone calls followed, and Roger was one of us.

May 12 and 13

John Seiter and I climbed Mt. Whitney up to about the 11,500 ft. elevation. Since we had no snow equipment, we didn't attempt to climb to the top. Neither one of us was in very good physical condition, and we realized that we needed a lot of work. We planned to climb some mountain on every possible weekend.

Mike Turnage, although now unable to exert himself physically, was still helping to organize and plan our coming trip to Ararat. Under his recommendation, we decided to enroll in a glacial mountaineering course on Mt. Hood, in Oregon. Mike, an experienced mountaineer and fantastic organizer, picked out all of the equipment and food that we needed.

May 16

John Bultema called and, after having read my letter and other material on the subject, reaffirmed his desire to go to Ararat, and he was accepted.

The trip was shaping up. We had four good men, each with his own good points, each with a different capacity to contribute. But we were still just a group of amateur mountaineers. None of us had had extensive training and experience in off-trail mountaineering.

May 27, 28, 29

John and I drove north, up through the giant redwood forests, to Kings' Canyon in California to continue our training. We did some camping and hiking, but very little climbing. Most of the time was spent at Hume Lake Conference Grounds, where we met many wonderful Christians vitally interested in our project and willing to help financially.

John Morris, from Virginia, and his favorite tree.

Seeing the sequoia trees was an uplifting and refreshing experience. The majesty and grandeur of these trees is even better appreciated when studied in light of the Biblical Flood. Some of these trees are estimated to be as much as 4000 years old. Where these trees are growing, there is no evidence of any previous generation of similar trees. Since these trees seemingly enjoy perpetual life (they are immune to disease and pest attack), it is reasonable to assume that some great catastrophe wiped out not only all living things in the area, but also all record of life shortly before the advent of these trees. Only the Great Flood in the days of Noah could meet these requirements. How exciting it was to think that we might play a part in reawakening scientists to the fact that Noah's Flood was indeed a historical event.

June 3

John Seiter and I climbed part way up San Gorgonio. Already the training was paying off. We were rounding into shape. We carried heavy packs, stuffed with any type of weight we could find, to strengthen our legs.

Mountain Lake, San Gorgonio, California.

June 4

A letter arrived from San Diego from Bill Ellison, a young man only 20 years old. Bill asked to join our group and listed impressive qualifications. He was a member of the San Diego Mountain Rescue Team, had taken several courses in rock climbing, as well as in mountain first aid, and seemed to be more mature than his age indicated. One letter and a few phone calls, and Bill was our fifth man.

June 7

Roger Losier, fresh from graduation exercises, arrived in L.A. bursting with energy and ready to go to work. Immediately he tackled the work of selecting proper equipment and food for our journey.

June 8

Eryl Cummings was in San Diego to visit my family and others. Roger and I drove down to share plans and information. Although he has been looking for Noah's Ark for years, he was willing to give me any information he could to aid us in the search. He could have withheld his information from me, but preferred to decrease his chances of making the discovery in hopes that the information might increase the chance of someone making it.

June 11

Roger and Bill left L.A. for Seattle, Washington. We had been granted an expedition discount from a large mountaineering store there. Roger was to buy enough dehydrated food to feed five men for ten weeks. Bill was to buy equipment.

June 22 thru 29

Roger and Bill drove from Seattle to Portland with all the equipmen and food. John Seiter and I drove up to Portland from Los Angeles. John Bultema flew from Michigan and, for the first time, all of us were together. We spent a week on Mt. Hood, near Portland, studying and practicing the art of glacial survival. We learned

Mt. Hood, near Portland, Oregon.

self-arrest techniques, crevasse rescue, use of equipment, etc., and climbed to the summit of the mountain on the last day (up the steep side).

All my life I have been called John. I've never had a nickname. Since three of us were named John, I suggested that we think up some nicknames, in hopes that I would get one. (The odds were 2 out of 3!) Right away, however, John Seiter revealed that many of his friends call him Skip, and John Bultema, claiming he didn't particularly like the name, agreed to sacrifice and offered to make J. B. his new title. That's the story of my life.

July 2 - Sunday

Skip and I are members of Van Nuys First Baptist Church in Los Angeles, probably the largest church on the west coast. We were called to the platform and, in front of thousands of people and over a large radio network, commissioned by the pastor to go search for Noah's Ark. (We had remained relatively unknown until then.)

10

Scott Memorial Baptist Church in San Diego, the church responsible for the founding of the Institute for Creation Research, commissioned us once again in the evening. Many of the church members contributed financially and many more offered their continued prayers. Four of us were present (J. B. had returned to Michigan), and it was comforting to know that so many wonderful and dedicated Christians were going to be remembering us in prayer throughout our trip.

July 5 - Wednesday

Again the four of us made a presentation, this time to Bill's home church. By this time, an air of elation had settled over us—we were actually on our way.

July 6 - Thursday

Finances were critical. We had spent all of the allotted money and still equipment and supplies needed to be purchased. Money trickled in all day from members of the church, and it seemed that there was always just enough to cover the purchases.

Roger, Skip, and I returned to Los Angeles well after midnight.

Chapter Two
Journey to the Center of the Earth

July 7 - Friday

After spending an extra day in San Diego, we had to rush all day long. Roger needed his second cholera shot, international driver's license, and personal clothing. I needed to verify the rental of the Hertz VW minibus in Turkey with the Auto Club, do some shopping, and purchase medicine and vitamins. Skip needed his shots validated, international driver's license, etc., and we all had personal business to clear up, not to mention the fact that we had to move out of the apartment. Some girls from church had invited us to a social on the beach, but, when we couldn't go, three of them came over, brought and cooked supper, cleaned up the kitchen, packed all the dishes in boxes and generally helped out. We could not have done without them. My family came over at 9:30 and with so many people in such a small apartment chaos reigned for a while, but after everyone settled down, it was ok. Roger had packed all the dehydrated food in boxes for shipment, and it was packed in the cars headed for San Diego, to be shipped to Turkey some time later.

Skip, Roger, and I put all our personal gear in our back packs until the weight was exactly 44 pounds, the weight limit allowed on international flights. The remainder of the gear was put in our ruck sacks and carrying cases which we would carry onto the plane. This, of course, included all the food, film, and cameras, which we didn't want to have X-rayed. The girls and my family left around midnight. Skip and I continued to pack until around 4 a.m.

July 8 - Saturday

After only two hours of sleep, we got up at 6 a.m. and showered and cleaned up. At 7 a.m., Skip's sister and brother-in-law and their children came over to pick up some of his stuff. At 7:30, Roger and I left in my car, and the others followed shortly in the other. My family and the Ellisons were waiting at the airport when we arrived and, again, chaos reigned. Everyone had something to worry about and it seemed that my leadership was not in question because they all came to me with their problems. Mrs. Ellison had $290 in cash and a $50 check which had been donated by their church, which she handed over to me. When everyone had arrived, we all checked in and proceeded to the boarding gate. As we approached, Skip felt that since we were carrying so much bulky, heavy, but important, gear with us as hand luggage, we ought to pray that we would be allowed to board without any trouble. So we did—right there in the busy Los Angeles airport we all huddled for prayer—the Morris's and the Ellisons, in-laws and friends, George Hillestad, and the four of us. Just that morning, President Nixon had issued an order that all hand luggage be searched, in an attempt to reduce the number of sky-jackings. Our luggage wasn't searched, although it did look very suspicious. Everyone was praying. The security officials objected only to our ice axes, which they packed in a box and stowed below. This was fine with us because they were very difficult and dangerous to carry.

Everyone realized that the Lord had undertaken and was guiding our trip. We praised Him for His goodness. We needed rest and got it on the flight to New York.

July 9 - Sunday

We flew through the night. Customs in New York searched Bill's hardware bag and removed some of the more dangerous pieces, but these were returned promptly in Frankfort. We had to

13

recheck all of our luggage there; no damage had been done and there were no problems. The airport in Frankfort is brand new, beautiful, and huge. There I found out that Skip had brought the little Minnex camera loaned to him by a friend in San Diego. We bought several rolls of film for it.

We were told that we could expect a stiff search when we boarded. The plane was an hour late and we were nearly the last to board. The officials took one look at the volume of equipment that we carried, simply frisked us, and allowed us to board.

Our flight to Beirut was unusual. We found out, much to our dismay, that the plane stopped in Istanbul with several possible Ankara connecting flights. But since we could not confirm any reservation and could not reroute our luggage, we reluctantly flew on to Beirut where we expected a day's layover. When we arrived, we found that it was a two-day layover.

The Beirut airport was a madhouse, as are so many of the facilities in the Arab world. The Customs officials in Beirut were checking everyone's luggage carefully, but when he saw our porter approach with five huge backpacks, five ruck sacks, five briefcases, clothing bags, stuff sacks, cameras, tents, etc., he simply turned his back until we passed by. After a lot of haggling with the porters, taxi drivers, and hotel clerks, we finally rented two rooms in the Cadmon's Hotel on the Mediterranean, the same hotel I had stayed in the year before. It was quite expensive for our budget pocketbooks, but we planned to charge the bill to J. B.'s American Express Card. After a word of prayer for guidance in the matter of airplane tickets, we went to bed.

July 10 - Monday

It took a long time to become accustomed to an 11-hour time change. We were all subject to fitful sleep and frequent naps. Maybe this was God's purpose in having us spend two days in Lebanon. Roger and I, rooming together, got up around 10 a.m., ate breakfast, and window shopped until noon when the others woke up. J. B., Roger, and Bill went sightseeing in the afternoon, but Skip didn't feel well and didn't go. I stayed behind to study Turkish, trying to refresh myself in that difficult language. My Turkish lessons had been completed over a month earlier and much had been forgotten. For supper, Skip and I had a Lebanese hamburger, which was perfectly terrible, and both of us were sick later that night. J. B., Roger, and Bill returned at 7:00 and had supper. Skip and Bill went right to sleep again. Roger and J. B. took an evening walk and I continued to study.

July 11 - Tuesday

Although I was being very careful about what I ate and drank, I was the first to come down with the tourista. It felt more like the flu than anything. We got up around nine (we still hadn't completely adjusted to the time change), ate breakfast, and took a walk in the market place. We had no money to buy anything, but it was fun. Although our flight out was at 6:30 in the evening, we left for the airport around three because the Customs officials had retained J. B.'s passport, and we needed time to reclaim it. I was feeling miserable throughout the entire ordeal. We noticed 13 burn spots on the plane parking apron, due to an Israeli raid two years ago, during which Israeli commandoes destroyed 13 airplanes. We arrived in Ankara, due to the time change, at 7 p.m., expecting to find a Hertz VW minibus waiting for us. To my horror, I found that it wasn't there, and, on the phone, Hertz officials advised us to check into a hotel, and they would send a representative to see us. Two expensive cabs took us to Ankara, and we checked into a very nice hotel (Stad Hotel). After supper, the Hertz representative came over and confessed that they had access to only one minibus, and furthermore that, since we had left the States, someone from the States had cabled to cancel our order. Their only minibus had been rented and was in use in another part of Turkey. He requested that we come to his office the next morning at eight.

After he left, Roger got upset and blamed me for our troubles, and I lost my temper. Bill shared with us something he had read about how the Lord always seems to work in mighty ways when the situation seems the most hopeless. We discussed the situation at length and made plans for the next day. In doing so, we grew closer together as a group. Roger and I apologized to each other. We had a long prayer session and went to bed around midnight.

July 12 - Wednesday

At 8 a.m. we arrived at the Hertz office, and by 8:30 the Hertz people were there. Over of a cup of cy (pronounced *chi*) tea, he explained that we couldn't have the minibus until the 23rd, and then only if we provided him with a detailed account of our plans. He tried to interest us in several other plans, none of which was acceptable: (1) rent two smaller cars; (2) rent one small car until the 23rd when we could have the minibus; (3) rent one old minibus until the 23rd. All of these plans were unacceptable, and, since we could not detail our itinerary, we assumed that the Lord had shut this door and had something better in store for us; but we had no idea of what that *something better* was and began following all logical avenues of progress. I called many car dealers, inquiring if they rented or not, and looking into the possibility of buying. In order to cover more ground, we split up. J. B., Roger, and Bill went to all of the car dealers that we had contacted. Most of these didn't speak English. Skip and I planned to go to the American hospital, which I thought was on the local American Air Force Base. We needed to acquire medicine and snake bite kits, in addition to searching for a suitable car for sale.

I had visited the Base the previous year and knew where to catch the Air Force shuttle bus. We started to get on the bus to the Base, but asked if it was going to the hospital. The driver said no, so we uncertainly got off. We noticed an American Air Force Sergeant on the other side of the street waiting for another bus, so we asked him how to get to the hospital. He said that the bus he was waiting for went there, and he would show us the way. The hospital is not on the Base, but in a different part of town. In the conversation that followed, we learned that he had just arrived that week from duty in the States. He had requested duty in Turkey because he had served once before in the southern Turkish city of Adona, location of a large American Air Force Base, and had grown to love the Turkish people.

The predominant religion in Turkey is Islam, and I knew that the preaching of Christianity is frowned upon, but I was still surprised by the sergeant's reaction to my next question. I asked if he happened to know a Christian friend of mine in Adona. He leaned over next to me and, in a lowered voice, told me about

16

several Christian men in Adona and asked whether I was a missionary. My inward doubt and despair turned to instant joy as we shared our common Christian testimonies.

There is nothing quite as exciting as being right in the middle of a miracle. While inwardly fighting back tears, I knew that the Lord was at that moment working a miracle and somehow was going to supply our needs through this man. We forgot the hospital and invited ourselves to his home for lunch. He didn't know our mission and had heard very little about the search for the Ark. It took some time for him to become interested but as we told him of our need, he jumped up, ran downstairs to the apartment bulletin board where we saw a simple 3x5 inch index card advertising a VW Minibus for sale. We called up the owner, Mike Ross, and within five minutes we were looking at the result of the miracle. Mike did not appear to know the Lord as his personal Saviour, although he was a devout Irish Catholic. In the conversation that followed, he seemed to be quite moved by our dedication and love for the Lord and was quite impressed by the fact that we considered him an answer to prayer. His car was clean and in

Our minibus - not much, but enough.

excellent running condition. We drove it around and then back to the hotel where he let us off. We planned to meet the next day around noon.

When Skip and I arrived back at the hotel and related the news, everyone's heart was encouraged. J. B., Bill and Roger had located a Turkish fellow who possibly would be willing to rent his Land Rover. He was coming by at 5 p.m. to inform us of his decision. Before he arrived, however, we had a prayer session, thanking God for supplying and asking Him to clearly show whether or not the Land Rover was to be used. When the man arrived, our prayers were answered. His first words were, "No, the Rover is not available."

That evening at six, we were guests at a pot-luck dinner at the Galatian Baptist Mission, a local fundamental church. The sergeant and his wife had insisted. Many believers were there who were vitally interested and willing to help us in any way possible. We ate good American food, sang many hymns, and had a wonderful time of fellowship with these people, all of them Service or Embassy personnel. Each of us gave a short testimony during the service. After church, the pastor took us to his home and told how he had attempted to climb Mt. Ararat. He related a tale of thieves, crooked officials, and mounting hardships that he and his friends had encountered attempting to climb the south face, the easy face.

The pastor informed us that under Turkish law it is nearly impossible for a tourist to purchase an automobile. So, in one evening, our spirits had been uplifted but our hopes diminished. One of the church members worked at the Embassy and offered to meet us there at nine the next morning to discuss the procedure of buying a car with their Customs expert.

Later, back in the hotel, we discussed the situation. Our conclusion was that the Lord had provided the car and He would provide a way to purchase it, just as He would supply the money with which to buy it.

July 13 - Thursday

We met at the Embassy at 9 a.m. and talked with the Customs official. He said that, although it is possible to make such a transaction in Ankara, there is so much red tape involved it might take up to two weeks. It would be easier to cross the border into either Syria or Greece and drive it back in under my name and passport.

From the Embassy, I talked with some friends of mine in Adona. They were looking forward to seeing us. The owner of the VW picked us up, and we drove to a VW dealer where the car was given a tune-up and checked over all. Mike somehow realized we were in the Lord's work and agreed to sell us the car for $1900 and throw in a complete set of new tires. We found a used luggage rack that we could have used but the owner wasn't around, so we went back to the hotel. Roger, J. B., and Bill had written letters all morning.

At 2 p.m., we rendezvoused at Mike's local bank to make financial arrangements for the sale of the car. J. B. had agreed to lend the money to the Institute and buy the car in my name. At the bank, he cashed a $250 check and at the American Express office he cashed another $500 check, the balance to be paid in cash and a bank draft from J. B.'s Michigan bank to the affiliated Irish Bank.

Roger and Bill visited the Hittite Museum that afternoon. After supper, J. B. and I took a walk in Genclik Park, which was quite refreshing. J. B., Skip, and I were still suffering from various diseases.

July 14 - Friday

We still needed medical supplies, so Skip and I went to the hospital that morning. On the shuttle bus, we again met a Christian, this time a nurse. One of the men from the church had agreed to give us the necessary supplies at no cost to us. The Lord continued to provide as we shopped in a nearby store, where we met an American professor with nothing to do but help us shop. After shopping, he took us to a VW dealer, which just happened to be the same one as before. This time, the owner of the luggage rack was there, but he refused to sell.

Each Friday the men of the little church have a prayer luncheon. We were invited and went. There, over hamburgers, some of the men told us of research that they had done in the past two days. They learned that it is impossible for any American to obtain a permit to climb Mt. Ararat. By this time, however, such news did not affect us — talk of impossible situations only increased our faith.

Mike Ross met us later back at the hotel. He had removed and returned his EY or Embassy license plates, a major obstacle to our buying his car, and replaced them with valid German plates. Throughout the day, J. B., Roger, and Bill had looked for a luggage rack but were unsuccessful; but with Mike and a student friend of his named Henry, from Teheran, Iran, we located and purchased a rack for 600 TL (About $50.00). With Henry's help, we bought more spare parts and unsuccessfully tried to get the title transfer notarized.

July 15 - Saturday

Mike was supposed to meet us at 8 a.m., but arrived at 9 a.m. He had been to a graduation party the night before and, because of the 11 p.m. to 4 a.m. curfew, had been unable to leave until 4 a.m. and was quite tired. All six of us then went to the American Embassy to utilize their notary services in the title transfer, but they are closed on Saturday. So we picked up another student friend of Mike's to interpret (his name was Atsu, from Cypress), and, while Skip, Roger, and Bill went once again to the hospital and shopping, J.B., Mike, Atsu, and I went to a notary. The notary typed out a full two-page report in Turkish, stamped it, and we were on our way. Next stop: the bank, where final payment was made. Then we transferred Mike's car insurance to my name. We could not have done all this without the help of Atsu.

We rendezvoused with Skip and the others, had lunch, checked out of the hotel, and began the long drive to Adona. (The hotel bill was $250.)

After several hours, we stopped for gas at a country station. Several men and boys came over and joked and kidded about our hair, sideburns, clothes, etc. It was a lot of fun. I was glad, for everyone's morale, that the people were so friendly, because many of the people of Ankara are not so friendly. We were all a little discouraged after spending so much time in Ankara.

The road to Adona is quite good, except for the last 100 kilometers which is through a mountain pass and very crowded, narrow, and dangerous. Skip drove through that at night. The pass had been called the Sicilian Gates throughout history and has been used by Alexander the Great, Roman armies, and others.

We checked into the Hotel OMUR, which was very cheap, and the rooms were small. There was no space in the rooms for our packs, and the hotel requested that we leave them outside on the bus, but we insisted that they be brought in. While we had committed the equipment to the Lord and asked Him to keep it safe, we still felt the need to take precautions.

July 16 - Sunday

We got up around 7:30 and, after showering in a primitive shower, Skip and I went over to see my friend Jack. We wandered around Adona looking for landmarks or street signs. Turkey does name its streets but does not always label them. It makes travel in a strange city most difficult. Luckily, we did find his place. He and his wife and little baby girl were just on their way to the Air Force Chapel for church. We agreed to meet again at 1:30, but when we returned to the hotel, we all decided to go to the Base. When the gate guards stopped us, Skip told them we were tourists and wanted to go to church. They called a chaplain, who escorted us onto the Base and into church. A Lutheran minister was preaching that week and a Negro soul group was supplying the music. Mike enjoyed the service, as did the rest of us. As the service ended, we saw Jack. He revealed his plans to cross the border also, to satisfy Customs' requirements for his family car, so we decided to go together. The chaplain invited us to lunch at the Officers' Club, and we gladly accepted. Eating Turkish food grows old fast, so we enjoyed the turkey dinner at the Club. The chaplain gave us a tour of the Base and showed us the CSA, supposedly the largest plane in existence.

Bill and I, and of course, Mike, were planning to go to Syria. We met at Jack's and, with two cars, began the trip. I drove about half the way, then let Mike drive while I rode with Jack. We talked of his work. He is a missionary of the Pentecostal Holiness Church and is trying to set up a Serviceman's Center in Adona. His wife works as a civilian on the Base. I told him all about our work and he became quite excited about it. We had a good time of fellowship.

As we neared the border, I got back in the van. The bord
crossing looked like a scene from the Twilight zone. The wi
was blowing hard and there was no moon. We were miles fro
any other houses that I could see. It was really quite spook
All of the border guards were on a cy break, except one wh
didn't speak English. After knocking heads for a long time,
guard arrived who spoke a little English. After much shouti
and misunderstanding, he finally passed both cars. The Turks a
very concerned about car smuggling. When a tourist such as Mil
drives a car into the country, it is stamped on his passport, and
must drive it out again. In order to sell it, the owner must dri
the car out of the country, and then the new owner must re-ent
with ownership papers, etc., and the car is stamped on his pas
port.

Twelve kilometers south of the Turkish Border gate is th
Syrian Border gate. It is called "Bab-el-Hava" or Gate of t
Wind," and it is aptly named. The wind was blowing so hard v
could hardly stand up. At the border, we had to buy visas ar
change money. The guard tried to short-change us, but we final
straightened things out. Next, we went to the adjacent buildin
Customs, where the car had to be checked. Only one fellow spok
English, and, while I was talking to him, a man came by with c
I thought it was for me and thanked him. Everyone laughed, b
the guard gave it to me anyway. The Turkish customs almost r
quire a businessman to serve his customers cy, and I thought th
same was applying here. I drank the cy, out of a dirty cup.
tasted horrible.

Bill drove into Aleppo. We had been told to stay in the Baro
Hotel, but could not find it. It was supposed to be a good on
We did find the Tourism Hotel, which was new and looked clear
and checked in — Jack and his family in one room, Bill and I i
another. Mike did not want to stay. His excuse was that it wa
too expensive, but I feel that he suddenly became lonesome fo
his wife, whom he hadn't seen for several weeks, and just didn
care to stay with strangers. We had witnessed to him all day an
the day before. We will continue to pray for him. After he lef
the four of us had a devotional in Jack's room before retiring.

July 17 - Monday

While eating our bread and honey, we made plans to visit hurriedly the Citadel in Aleppo and leave town, but as we were checking out I found that my traveler's checks were no good and I needed to exchange them for Syrian money to pay the bill. I was taken to a local bank. The Arabs are fine people, but tend to be disorganized and unbelievably involved in red tape. It took over an hour to change $10, and, by the time it was done, I was frustrated and our sightseeing time was gone.

Crossing the Syrian Border took time. They had just opened and a lot of people were waiting in line. But we had no problems. We did have problems at the Turkish gate. It seems these officials can make up their own rules as they see fit. Furthermore, no one there spoke any English. Jack was not allowed to transfer title to his wife's passport as he had hoped. They demanded that I return to the same gate that I had crossed the day before. (We had gone to another, hoping it would look less conspicuous.) But my limited Turkish finally wore them down, and, tired of trying to make me understand, they allowed us into the country.

We drove back without a meal and stopped at Jack's for supper. It is about a 7-hour drive. We planned to take a month's supply of food with us when we went to Eastern Turkey and leave the rest with Jack. Jack indicated a desire to see Mt. Ararat and was willing to drive out with the rest of our supplies in about a month.

When Bill and I returned to the hotel, we found that the three others had purchased a tarp and some tires during the day, so they left to have them installed.

July 18 - Tuesday

Jack invited us to his house for breakfast at eight. After breakfast, we shopped for incidental items, picked up the tarp, packed the car, and left around 1 p.m.

Skip recommended that I delegate authority more, instead of trying to do everything myself. That was very good advice. Immediately I put J. B. in charge of financial records and Roger in charge of packing the car for the remainder of the trip. I planned to do more of that as the chance arose.

The car was heavily loaded. As we drove toward more rural areas, the people became increasingly friendly. J. B. gets special pleasure out of being called a "haji," or holy man, because of his beard. He has a pleasant personality and people instantly like him. The roads are not always paved in this section of Turkey, but we drove on. At dusk, we were literally pulled off the street in the city of Malatya by a hotel clerk who set us up with nice rooms at a reasonable rate. People were all very curious and friendly.

July 19 - Wednesday

We were in a hurry to get to our destination. We were on the road by 9 a.m., taking turns driving over terrible roads, but through beautiful country. Central and Eastern Turkey are made up of rugged mountain ranges. The Great African Rift, a major earthquake fault, runs through the middle of Turkey, and earthquakes are common here; consequently, the mountains are very rugged and the geology is striking. On dirt and gravel roads most

Streets of Igdir.

24

of the day, our engine began to lose power and one headlight was broken.

As we neared Erzerum, we decided not to stay in the same hotel that Eryl Cummings and his party usually stay in, just to avoid any possible trouble. But the situation was a little different than we supposed. All of the good or semi-good hotels were filled, and the only room we could find was in an inferior hotel, a filthy place with one filthy toilet per floor. The rooms were small and we asked for a garage where our equipment would be safe. One kid was there who in broken English stammered that his dad was a "garaj polis" and we could park in his alley. He even had a rubber stamp with the word "garaj" on it. We decided not to use his services and unloaded the car, took all our stuff upstairs, and parked the car on the sidewalk.

July 20 - Thursday

The hotel was so filthy, several of us preferred to be dirty rather than take cold showers there. After our morning devotional, I walked down to the hotel where Eryl Cummings usually stays and was informed at the desk that he was not in town. From the desk clerk I obtained the address of a good VW mechanic and found an auto parts store.

While we stood on the sidewalk, a teacher from Ataturk University, who spoke very good English, offered to take us to the auto mechanic and interpret and bargain for us. The mechanic was very busy and couldn't work on the car until 1:30. So Memket, our new-found friend, showed us a good restaurant and left.

The Lord never seems to do anything important when we expect it or try to predict it. Once again, at breakfast, He surprised us. We met a Turkish sergeant, stationed near Mt. Ararat, who was most friendly. He was in the company of several officers. He invited us to visit him if we ever in our "tourist travels" visited that area. We all felt that he would play an important role in the weeks to come.

On the street we met two fellows who, due to a lack of communications, seemed to indicate that they worked for an auto parts store. They offered to fix the broken headlight. Soon it was evident that they didn't even know which end of a screwdriver to use, let alone how to fix a headlight. Skip fixed them in spite of the two fellows, although we never did get the parking lights to work.

We were checking out of the hotel and preparing to take the car to the mechanic when Memket, the professor, popped up again. He took Skip and me to his home to shower and clean up. While there, we told him about Christianity and how it compares to Islam. He was quite receptive, especially when we told him of assurance of salvation and forgiveness of sins, two features lacking in Islam. As a gift, he gave Skip a copy of the Koran. He is a wonderful fellow. After showering, Skip and I walked to the garage and found the car almost ready.

After an early supper, we began the long drive to Igdir. The mountains we passed through were beautiful. There seemed to be a layer of chalk or gypsum underlying lava, with many granitic intrusions. The whole area has been folded and faulted until everything is crushed and crumpled.

In Igdir we checked into another very dirty hotel. It seemed that everyone in town crowded around and caused quite a stir. After supper in an outdoor restaurant, we went to bed with the lice.

Chapter Three

The Mountain
and the Men

July 21 - Friday

I had been doing a lot of thinking about our approach to the mountain. Mr. Cummings had said that we needed a permit to climb, but we had found many things different than he had thought. Our general policy of this trip, and in fact of our Christian life, is to submit to and follow local law. But on the chance that a permit would not be required, I decided that we should attempt to drive up to the mountain without one. If we were turned back, fine; we would then seek to secure one. In this manner we would try all possible avenues in the correct order.

I informed the fellows of this intention and stated also that, in all probability, we would be coming back to Igdir frequently for supplies and rest. So we spread out, just bumming around town, buying small things and in general being friendly to the local townspeople. The people of Igdir are very friendly, and we were as well received as we had been anywhere. We saw the Mountain for the first time from the hotel window, a most impressive sight.

We left town around noon, driving between the mountain and the Russian border. I had been told that the road on that side of the mountain was forbidden without a permit, and as we cautiously proceeded we were encouraged by the lack of military personnel and roadblocks, etc. Actually, there was nothing preventing our progress. At one point we passed a military base or post.

The guards were playing soccer in a nearby field. They simply waved at us as we went by. After seeking directions several times to Ahora, we were finally directed to a dirt path leading out over the plain toward the mountain.

The afternoon was cloudy and hazy, and I could not directly recognize the gorge at Ahora and, therefore, could not get my bearings for a while. The road was cluttered with rocks of all sizes and was uphill all the way. The VW had trouble pulling the grade with all the weight, and occasionally we had to get out. Several times the road disappeared and we had to hunt for it. Once we ran into a village with absolutely no one in it. Everyone —men, women, and children were apparently up on the mountain tending sheep. We continued on uncertainly until we arrived at Ahora.

Ahora is on a grassy hill overlooking the largest of the drainage streams flowing out of the gorge itself. Evidently in previous years,

Base Camp at Ahora.

28

one could drive a car across the stream directly into Ahora, but the road had been washed out. There was a nice place to camp right between the road and the stream, in full sight of Ahora, but while we were considering it, about 10 Kurdish men and boys came over, so we began looking for a place with more privacy. We found one just over the hill. Several boys helped us clear rocks while the men sat down and watched us, including the "Muhtar" (Mayor) of Ahora. He was most friendly and helpful, assuring us that we could camp anywhere, climb the mountain, and do anything we wanted. We set up camp near a small but dirty stream, the two tents next to the bus.

After supper, we had a time of Scripture reading and prayer together. We established "The Church of Ararat" by reading the entire Flood story from Genesis and even sang a few hymns. We all felt very close to the Holy Spirit, realizing that now we were finally in a position to actually do the work God had called us to do, and that we had not been able to do any of this work in our own strength. We planned to spend the entire next day acclimatizing and resting for the climbs ahead.

All of us except Skip had gone to bed when we got our first real taste of Kurdish hospitality. The mayor and two of his friends decided to pay us a friendly visit — only they brought their guns and were not at all friendly. They informed us that we would have to leave the next morning, go to the military, and get a permit. They were not speaking in English, or in very good Turkish for that matter, and it was hard to understand. They were hollering and screaming and none of them had any teeth, so any good my Turkish lessons had done was nullified. I knew what they wanted but acted as if I didn't, hoping they would tire and leave, but when they started talking about *shooting* and *hanging,* I decided to understand.

There are many different military posts near the base of Ararat. Not all of them have jurisdiction over any part of Mt. Ararat but several of them do. "Muhtar" indicated that we were to go to an outpost that I did not even know existed and would never have thought to go there looking for a permit to climb Mt. Ararat. So it seemed that the Lord used a direct method to inform us of the location of the Army Commander with the power to issue permits. (I did not know the names of the different military bases but since this was the eighth* I had come in contact with, I refer to it as Base 8.)

July 22 - Saturday

The dimensions of Turkey are rather large, especially in the East-West direction. But the entire country is in one time zone, which fits Western Turkey. Consequently, in Eastern Turkey the sun comes up around 3 a.m.

We were still in bed at 4 when a man came by to check and see if we were still there. We assured him we would leave shortly. At 7, the local religious leader came by and introduced himself as "Pastor." We talked for about an hour. He claimed that he was placed in Ahora under salary by the government. When he offered to go to town with us and help obtain the permit, we gladly accepted, knowing that the language barrier would be hard to overcome without him.

Adem Urnal, our new-found friend, was a wonderful person, pleasant and extremely easy to talk to, in Turkish, of course. He left our camp but soon returned, clean-shaven and in an attractive suit. Skip, the Pastor, as we began calling him, and I drove into town to acquire that impossible permit, leaving about 9 a.m.

That morning I had awakened with a vicious backache. I could not stand erect and pain accompanied each movement. Once before, while mountain climbing in California, I had had this same problem. I did not understand why the Lord had decided to cripple me in such a way, but accepted it, knowing that He must have had a reason.

Once in Base #8, at the Army headquarters, we enjoyed cy with an Army sergeant and several civilians, one of whom was the Mayor of a nearby village. But they could not help us and sent us to the man who could. We had to wait in the hall for a few minutes, and, as we did, a young man of about 16 introduced himself in English and offered his small talents as an interpreter. But, despite his help and the pleadings of Pastor, the Commander told

---

*Author's note: This was the eighth of eleven bases that we observed, but no doubt there are many more. The Russian border is only a few kilometers away and the area is heavily patrolled.)

us emphatically no, that Americans were not allowed on Mt. Ararat, due to an agreement between Turkey and Russia. Over more cy he agreed to give use permission to climb from another side. By this time a crowd had gathered, among them a boy of 12 who spoke very good English. With his help, I told the Commander that women and children climb from the other side, while only men could climb in the gorge, and that we didn't want to climb to the top but only halfway up. He consented to give us two days, under several conditions, but finally stretched it to one week, probably because, in my weakened condition, he realized that I couldn't even climb stairs. This didn't seem like much time but we realized that if that was all the time we had, then the Lord must have thought that was all we needed.

Outside we bought some watermelons and a water can which we filled from the spring. Water is always critical.

Back on the rocky road to Ahora, I asked the Pastor if he could arrange it with the Mayor for us to stay two weeks instead of one, but he said no. At camp we made plans for the next day. A one-day reconnaissance was planned. Four of the group (all except me) would climb up on the east side of the gorge and search the west side with the field glasses and telescopic lenses. They planned to leave at dawn.

We had a nice supper and were preparing for bed when the Pastor and the Mayor slipped into camp, this time without guns. The Mayor was all smiles. He offered to let us stay for two weeks and, in the same breath, asked for Skip's watch. We promised him the watch in two weeks. Finally, they left and we finished packing and went to bed.

July 23 - Sunday

Several years ago, while descending the mountain after a couple of weeks of searching, Eryl Cummings and Bud Crawford (of Search) had taken many random telephotos in the Ahora Gorge region. Much later, while studying the slides, he noticed an object way off in the distance that seemed to fit the general description of the Ark given by eyewitnesses. It appeared to be a barge-like structure, protruding from a grayish snow bank, capped by a catwalk extending its entire length. All who have seen the picture agree that it must be re-located and photographed in detail, but the field of vision is so small it is impossible to determine exactly where on the mountain that object rests. The only thing that can be said for sure is that the picture was taken from the east side of the Ahora Gorge looking at the west side.

As the men set out that morning, their instructions were to climb the grassy slopes on the east side of the gorge and, with field glasses and telescopes, search the rugged west side. We hoped to re-locate the object in Cummings' picture from a distance and climb to it in the following days.

As was our custom, we prayed as a group before splitting up, asking the Lord for safety, guidance, and unity within the group; but within ten seconds of the "Amen," the unity was gone. Bill, our most experienced climber, but the newest member of our group, began passing out petty orders and tempers flared. As they were walking away, I realized that Bill might not realize that Skip was in charge, so I reminded him. No more was said but it was obvious that feelings were hurt and relations strained.

Left alone in camp, I prepared my pack for the next day's climb. I had hoped that Skip, Bill, and I could climb the west side of the gorge and look down in it from above. I expected the climbers to find that object from a distance, giving us some direction in our search.

Throughout the day, a steady stream of visitors harangued me. I could not speak well enough to carry on a meaningful conversation, so we conversed on a very low and repetitious level. First, the Pastor came by. He is a nice guy but overstays his welcome. He has nothing to do during the day when most of the men are working. Pastor finally left but was replaced by Mayor. In broken Turkish, he informed me that a friend of his was in jail in a nearby town, and he wanted to go get him out. The kicker was that he wanted to use our minibus. I told him "no" many times. His hands and eyes were continuously roving around and he asked for everything he touched. Finally he left, his feelings hurt, but I could not relax.

Pastor returned. I offered him fruit punch, and, while we were drinking, he told me of an old Armenian monastery that had stood on the very site of our camp. It had been destroyed by an earthquake and subsequent flood. But an Armenian graveyard remained nearby and he showed it to me. It was definitely Christian, all the tombstones had crosses and candlesticks on them. He mentioned an old Russian graveyard within a few miles. As we walked, he told me about the Koran and its laws and how sin cannot be forgiven. By using the symbol of the cross, I tried to explain that by the death of Jesus our sins are forgiven, and I think he got the message. Soon he left, but once again the Mayor and a friendly young man reappeared. After sharing a watermelon, they demanded everything from binoculars to booze. Any kind of alcohol, whisky, beer, raki, and any pill or hashish was okay. They were most obnoxious. Over and over again I explained that I had none, but their demands increased. Again the Mayor wanted to use the car. After about two hours of arguing, I decided that the only way to make them understand was to get mad. So I screamed and hollered, shook my fist, threw my hat on the ground, and generally told him that if he didn't shut up I'd knock his head off. Would you believe it? He understood and quickly left. Throughout the day, other men dropped by, most of whom I

Mt. Ararat and the Ahora Gorge.

33

had never seen before. They all wanted to see and handle everything. It took real diplomacy to ward them off and remain on good terms.

In the early afternoon, Roger entered camp by himself. As I had feared, Satan had disunified the group. Roger had been separated from the group because neither he nor Bill could overcome their pride. Roger is a fast walker and has a habit of walking ahead of the others and waiting until they catch up before starting out again. But once he sat down to wait and found himself alone. Bill, behind him, had chosen another route and had abandoned him. Neither would signal the other. Skip evidently had given leadership to Bill and approved of this action. It is very dangerous for one person to be alone in an area as lawless as this. But when Skip returned, he had a long talk with Roger and things were straightened out.

The climb had not been particularly successful. The day was hot and soon all four had run out of water. While J. B. and Skip rested and scoured the other side of the gorge at about 10,000 ft.

Upper reaches of the west side of the Ahora Gorge.

elevation, Roger and Bill continued up to about 11,500 ft. They searched for water and finally found a small spring. After trying and failing to reach the edge of the gorge, they returned to the others with the water and soon it was time to descend to camp. They did, however, locate some pillow lava (dense, hard lava usually with conchoidal fractures, formed only by extrusion under great depths of water), important in geologic studies, demonstrating the fact that the mountain was once covered by many thousands of feet of water.

All four were very tired. Neither Bill, Skip, nor J. B. expressed any desire to resume climbing the next day. And we only had one week. I had hoped that they would see the "object," but they didn't. It would be futile to try and climb to the upper reaches of the mountain without knowing where to go. I have felt all along that, although our experience and knowledge are seriously limited, our potential is great. So the Lord Himself must guide and show us what He wants us to see.

After studying the mountain, it seemed that Cummings' picture might have been taken from a low vantage point, So, with this direction, Roger and I made plans to enter the gorge itself to try and find the object. This, we thought, was very dangerous, due to rockslides which we had heard frequently throughout the day.

The Pastor and three other men who had been hanging around for several hours finally left but returned with a young friend just in time for supper. So we had to ration out the food and offer them some. After supper, the young fellow filled our water jug with spring water. It was much better water than we had been drinking.

To avoid offending the Pastor, Skip and I accepted his invitation to tea at his place, even though we were tired and needed sleep. Several hours and many cups of tea later, they let us go.

Chapter Four
"Object" Hunting in Ahora Gorge

July 24 - Monday

Although we had only been gone two weeks, everyone wanted to wrap it up and go home. We were not discouraged and did not want to quit, but didn't want to waste any time either. We were tiring of the constant stress of living in a strange country, surrounded by strange circumstances and people. So as Roger and I left for the gorge at 5 a.m., we were spurred on by those thoughts.

As we walked, I remembered the comments of the men the day before and the men on previous expeditions. All had agreed that the mountain is bigger than it looks . . . and now I agreed. We walked for about ten miles before even reaching the beginning of the gorge itself. We tried to follow donkey trails as much as possible, but frequently there were no trails and we were forced to cross over huge boulder fields. All the rocks and boulders had been washed out of the gorge during floods or had fallen off surrounding slopes in avalanches. All were loose and very dangerous.

Near the true entrance to the gorge is a small Kurdish camp composed of about ten families, all living in tents. We had been walking for several hours when we entered this village. All the men, women, and children were off tending their flocks of sheep and goats and the town was nearly deserted. At one point two

Kurdish family at their summer home.'

dogs attacked us, one from each side. We had no trouble holding them off, but were not able to advance. The owner of these fierce animals ran out and called them off and invited us into his tent for tea. We needed the rest and accepted his hospitality. He had 15 kids under the age of 10, or so it seemed. Some red-haired and freckle-faced and some dark. All were cute, but dirty and poorly dressed. The lady of the house was busy making yogurt and offered us some, dipping her hand into the churn and bringing out a handful. Perhaps it was her sister or possibly her daughter, but a teen-age girl kept peeking around the tent poles or rugs at Roger and me. The man kept saying something about her that I didn't quite understand, but it sounded like a proposal of marriage. Our ignorance of the language once again proved that "ignorance indeed is bliss."

Just beyond the village is a steep hill, a climb of about 1000 feet. The tea in the village upset my stomach, and by the time we climbed that slope, I was sick. We walked into the gorge for several hours before stopping for lunch, searching the sides of the

37

gorge with binoculars continually. The man from the village had accompanied us this far and we shared lunch with him. He didn't like our trail food any better than we liked his yogurt. He didn't even eat the chocolate bar. Roger and I had been drinking water frequently and perspiring profusely, until we noticed that our friend did neither. He never took more than a swallow of water. Thinking that he may know something, we cut down on our intake and felt much better.

We climbed up to a flat place on the western wall of the gorge and studied the eastern. Almost immediately we saw "the object," that thing in Cummings' picture. It was on a ledge adjacent to a finger glacier running from the top of the gorge through a heavy landslide area and down to the bottom. We seemed to be looking at its end, for it seemed to extend back into a snow bank. It had the shape of a barge, with a center piece running from top to bottom of a different color. It was tan with brown top and center piece, but from our distant vantage point it looked small compared to its surroundings, much less than 450 feet in length. Both Roger and I were very excited and moved in for a closer look.

Roger Losier (part mountain goat) inside the Ahora Gorge.

Every afternoon on Mt. Ararat the evaporation from the plains below collects and condenses on the mountain. First, the gorge gets hazy, then the clouds form on the peak, and by nightfall the entire mountain is covered with clouds. As we walked toward our "object," the haze set in. Soon the sun was darting in and out of the clouds. When the sun was behind a cloud we couldn't even distinguish our "object" from rocks in the area, even though we were looking right at it. As we approached it, we speculated, as the haze permitted, that the object was a rock and part of the entire shelf. Furthermore, we realized there was not enough room in that area for a ship the size of Noah's Ark, nor was the object large enough to qualify. To actually reach the site would require many hours of rugged climbing through an area subject to rock slides every minute. The object itself was continually pummeled with rocks from above. A wooden structure could not have survived a summer's day, let alone 5000 years. So, even though we were not able to see the object up close, we ruled it out as a possibility based on these several good reasons; but it never left the back of my mind. I made plans to see it from above.

While trying to get a better look at the object, we had walked to the very end of the gorge. Most of the way we followed a creek bed. There was no trail and we hopped from boulder to boulder, all of them loose and moving. Earlier, as we walked we passed many shepherds and their flocks grazing on the grass and flowers growing in between the rocks. But as the terrain got rougher we were alone. At the end of the gorge, there is a huge and foreboding black glacier, full of holes and crevasses. It is solid ice but black as coal. As it moves, it picks up lava dust and is completely impregnated with it. At the far end of this black glacier is a beautiful waterfall possibly 300 feet in height, fed by the melting ice and snow above. Surrounding the black glacier, snow is piled perhaps 100 feet in some places, but it is not noticeable unless one digs down through the rock and dust cover. Avalanche rock debris has completely covered the snow.

I cannot overemphasize the effect of these avalanches. They sound like thunder and can be heard for miles. They affect your ability to search because you must constantly keep a sharp lookout on all nearby slopes while climbing on, over, and through the debris left by previous avalanches, and, of course, progress is

39

Avalanch debris in Ahora Gorge. Note the rare black glacier.

slow due to the obstructions; but most of all, you're just plain scared. When rocks are falling all around and mobility is limited, the natural human response is fear, not panic, just fear.

Once we had come to the conclusion that our "object" was not the Ark, and the decision to climb to the west side of the gorge had been made, we turned around and headed back to camp. In the late afternoon all the flocks of sheep had been returned to their folds and no one except Roger and I were in the gorge. We saw no one until we entered the village near the entrance to the gorge that we had previously passed through. Roger was walking ahead of me, and as he slid down the slope into the village one dog attacked him, but Roger held him off. Our friend who had earlier given us tea came out, called off the dog and welcomed Roger.

Soon I slid in and again the dog attacked, but in the company of the village I was safe; however, the dog continued to bark and

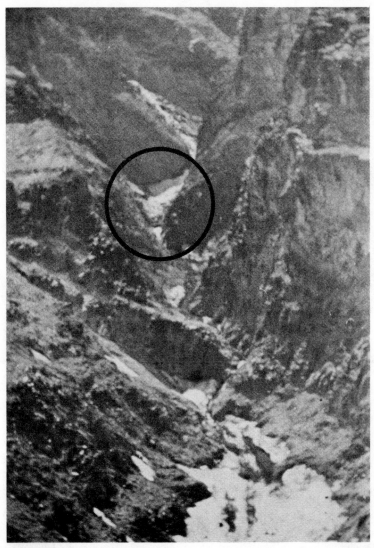

Our "object", resting on the edge of the Ahora Gorge, the most rugged
area of Mt. Ararat.

made a lot of racket from a distance. This aroused every dog in town, all of whom had returned from a day's work in the fields. The man invited us in again, but we declined and walked on.

Before we knew it, dogs were everywhere. These are Kurdish wolfhounds, half dog and half wolf. About ten dogs surrounded us, wolf style. They continually tightened the circle, moving in for the kill. Roger and I stood back to back with a rock in each hand, trying to scare them away. We did not dare throw the rocks, because then we would have had no rocks to throw. Several were drooling and foaming at the mouth, and all were ready for blood. But just as the dogs closed their circle to a radius of about five feet, another man came over and with a big stick began beating his own three dogs off. This broke up the circle and Roger and I ran for an open spot. Once the dogs were all in front of us we shouted and threw rocks until they scattered. With a quick "thanks" to the stranger, we started off at a fast walk, pausing only long enough to throw rocks at the pursuing dogs. Once again the Lord had brought us through an impossible situation, and as soon as we were alone we thanked Him.

We were still many miles from camp. I was tired and rather sick from the tea given us that morning, but Roger, who is part

Entrance to the Ahora Gorge. Note Kurdish village at bottom of slope in center. Site of wolf dog attack.

mountain goat, was still fresh. About two miles from camp, two friends from Ahora approached us and one of them finally convinced me to ride his horse. Now, I am less of a horseman than a mountaineer, and it was hard to decide which method of travel was more tiring.

When we entered camp about dusk everyone was worried. They got quite a kick out of seeing me ride the horse. During supper, I informed J. B., Skip, and Bill of their task for the remainder of the week. They had anticipated the same and were nearly packed.

Bill suggested that they not take a tent the following week. He said he wanted to "bivouac in." Skip agreed. Since Bill was the most experienced climber of all, and I was the most inexperienced, I did not overrule this decision, even though it all sounded strange.

Many Turks were in camp, including the Mayor, just returned from town. He had with him a man just released from jail and was quite proud of the part he played in his release. I told all of the Turks I was sick and they left in a hurry. They must have thought it was contagious.

July 25 - Tuesday

Soon after dawn, J. B., Bill, and Skip started out. It was very disconcerting to see them leave without a tent but I said nothing. After they left, Roger and I went back to bed for several hours.

We spent the day fighting flies and mosquitoes, entertaining visitors, and dodging the sun. We erected a tarp system to provide some shade, but could not avoid the Kurds. All of them wanted to talk and pass the time of day under our tarp. They were friendly, but handled everything, asking how much it cost and if they could have it. They could not be left alone.

Both Roger and I were able to bathe and wash clothes in the only clean stream around. There are only a few places on all the mountain where the water is fit to drink, but even then it must be treated. The mountain is covered with lava dust and other sediments, and water, as it flows, becomes filthy.

July 26 - Wednesday

More of the same—hot sun, scores of flies, continous company. "Muhtar" the Mayor again haunted the camp. Roger couldn't stand it and left. After listening for hours to him asking for everything, I blew my stack. It must have looked funny, but I imitated him gawking and begging for every object in our bus. He got the message and acted like a hurt little boy. He sat on a rock and sulked for a long time, then left without a word. I didn't want to ruin our relationship and certainly didn't want to act un-Christian, but what else could I do? He has such a low mentality and our speech is so limited.

Clouds covered the mountain around dusk and prepared to rain or snow. We estimated that the three climbers were on top of the glacier and prayed for their safety.

July 27 - Thursday

It had rained constantly throughout the night and temperatures were cool. The mountain was covered with clouds most of the day, but when they receded we could see that some snow had fallen, although not enough to affect the search. The day was cool and much more pleasant than the previous two.

During the morning, I read the entire book of Exodus, noting that many of my personal feelings of inadequacy in the area of leadership were the same that Moses felt; but the Lord saw fit to use him in spite of his weaknesses. The Israelites had many problems because they took their eyes off the Lord and His provisions and began to look at their immediate surroundings. Our problems as a group seemed to stem from the same source. The entire morning was well spent.

There is a stream that runs near our campsite. It is muddy and undrinkable, and the flow varies throughout the day. Far up the mountain the Kurds divert the flow into irrigation canals to water their flocks and keep the grass growing. This is one of the few industrious undertakings of the Kurdish community.

The Kurds, for most of the day, gave us a break. With the exception of Muhtar, they stayed away. Again I was forced to be stern with him and send him away, but this is their land and we are guests. I wish they would act like good hosts.

July 28 - Friday

The morning brought more threatening weather, cool and humid after raining most of the night. In the afternoon, the mountain was very cloudy, and I was worried about the men on top. I hoped they would not lose their bearings in the fog.

Only a few visitors graced our camp. One of these was the Mayor, of course. He came to remind us that our week was almost up. Earlier, he had told us to stay two weeks, in hopes of receiving some gift. We promised him a watch at the end of the period, but I think he just wanted to go to town with us, so was forcing us to leave.

In mid-afternoon, Skip, J. B., and Bill returned to camp, exhausted and out of sorts. I had not hoped for overwhelming results, but the story of their climb flabbergasted me.

Day 1: They were carrying heavy packs and were not able to go as far as they had hoped. Bill complained of lack of energy and was very slow. The other two had to assist him with his load and hired a local Kurdish boy to help him as he walked. So they halted progress on a grassy slope about halfway between base camp and their anticipated destination. They had run out of water during the day and twice received some from local children. Near their new camp was a snowbank from which they extracted water for their meals.

Day 2: They were without a tent and slept out in the open. In the morning, Skip woke up with one of the vicious Kurdish dogs looking him straight in the eye. Luckily, the dog lost interest and returned to his sheep. As they prepared for departure, a bunch of Kurdish kids surrounded them and tried to steal things and begged for money. They pestered the men until Skip ran them off with his ice-ax, but from a distance the kids threw rocks with surprisingly good aim. Bill felt better and progress was good that morning. Later, as they walked through a Kurdish village (despite the dogs and the kids), a woman ran up to them holding a dead baby in her arms. They supposed she wanted medicine or money, but all they could give was sympathy. They climbed up the grassy slopes and across large boulder fields until they reached the bottom of a finger glacier extending up to the ice-cap. Here they camped and made plans to climb the finger the next day. Water was plentiful but still they had no shelter, so they spread out their ground cloth and slept on it; however, it rained all night, and they and their gear were soaked. Down sleeping bags provide absolutely no protection or warmth when wet. They were very cold and did not sleep much.

Day 3: The most immediate problem was taking care of their gear. They tried to dry it out on nearby rocks but small showers throughout the day hindered. The weather was fairly good in the morning but Skip thought it best not to attempt the climb. Most of the day was spent building a shelter. They dug a snow cave, built up the sides with rocks, and covered it with their ground cloth and Bill's parka — but it rained again that night and all were drenched.

Day 4: The morning weather was adequate, but rather than climb with only one day of food left Skip decided to return to camp. As they descended, J. B., spotted an object on the upper slopes that appeared to be handmade. The object seemed to be a long vessel, broken in two places with an oval hatch beside it. The clouds frequently hid it but they took pictures and studied it as best they could. They did not try to get any closer since it was some distance away. Continuing their descent, they had several encounters with kids and dogs, but reached base camp at 3 p.m.

*   *   *

As they related their stories to me, I sensed friction between them. I did not understand why, but the feeling was unmistakable. Satan was again trying to destroy our unity and effectiveness.

We discussed the possibilities for the future. We had to choose between remaining in Ahora and hoping that the Mayor would extend our permit, or go back to town and attempt to secure another one. J. B. and Roger wanted to remain if the Mayor would allow, even though we would be at his mercy and without hopes of jandarma protection. Bill wanted to leave, search for ruins at the foot of the mountain, and return later. Skip had no strong feelings either way, but all of them left the decision up to me. I spent many sleepless hours that night.

Chapter Five
Archaeological Interlude

July 29 - Saturday

The Mayor had promised to stop by in the morning to discuss our plans, but he didn't, so Skip and I went to see him at noon. He said we could stay another week or leave for a week and return with no permit. He seemed almost anxious to have us around without permission.

So I made my decision, based on the following observations: I knew of the Mayor's greed and felt that possibly he would try to rob us if we stayed without official permission. There was a good deal of unrest among us, and a few days in town away from these people might give us a chance to regroup. We could try to re-locate ruins of the shrine at the base of the mountain. We could attempt to obtain another permit from the authorities, but if unable to obtain one, we could return and try the Mayor's hospitality. I decided we would leave the mountain that day, try to re-locate the ruins at Karadag from the other side of the mountain, apply for an additional permit, and, most of all, regain our unity before returning.

We were packing our bus when a truck drove up. Some of the Kurds had told us a group of thirty tourists were several miles

47

away climbing the mountain. But this group represented the Turkish Highway Department and were contemplating mapping the dirt road to Ahora. What a joke!

We checked into the Hotel Asya in Igdir. It is supposed to be the best in town, but is nothing to brag about. We shopped for insect repellent, etc., and just bummed around. Roger and J.B. had met a boy named Ulmus last time we stayed in Igdir. He claimed to know where Karadag was located, but his directions were nebulous, so we agreed to take him along when we went the next day.

July 30 - Sunday

In 1905, an officer in the White Russian Army located an archaeological site of possible great significance. He thought, according to his writings, that the area was constructed and abandoned by the original inhabitants of the area the first few generations after the Flood. The most important discovery was a rock with both pictorial and cuneiform writing on it. The officer had translated the carvings. According to his translation, they told in part the story of the Flood and described Mt. Ararat as the final resting place of the Ark. The name of the mountain at that time was Karadag. Mr. Cummings, in his investigations, had met the old man and received from him many maps and sketches of the area.

The old maps located Karadag in a remote area, a rugged lava flow, many miles from civilization of any kind. The nearest road is the gravel highway stretching from Igdir to Dogubeyazit and over a mountain pass. Our incomplete map indicated a trail going off the main road toward the area of search.

At dawn, Ulmus, our young friend, met us at the hotel. J. B., Roger, and I were the only ones going to Karadag, Bill and Skip preferring to remain in Igdir. Our "guide" directed us on to several wrong roads before we finally found the one to Dogubeyazit. It wasn't long before I concluded that not only did he not know the location of Karadag, he didn't even know the way out of town, but he was helpful as an interpreter, so we kept him — besides, he got a kick out of riding in the bus.

The highway was being repaired. We found a very nice gravel road leading in the right direction, but it ended abruptly. A construction crew was standing around, doing very little. The road

Streets of Dogubeyazit. Note: no women.

had not yet been completed and, from the looks of the crew, it would be a while. (I pity the Turkish Highway Commission when someone finds the Ark. They will try to turn the area into a tourist attraction, I'm sure, but first they had better hire skilled labor.) We could not pass and decided to try to reach the area from the other side . . . so, back to the main road, over the mountain pass, through the woods, to Grandmother's house we went, but on the other side things were worse. No construction had been attempted, and the road was made for an automobile no bigger than a donkey. Time was slipping by, so we gave up.

Last year, my tour group had stayed in a certain hotel in Dogubeyazit, on the southern side of Mt. Ararat. At the time, I was appalled at the filthy accommodations and bad food, but everything is relative, and when we ate lunch there it looked like a palace, with excellent cuisine. When compared to what we had been used to, anything would look good.

East of Dogubeyazit are the ruins of an old walled fortress, abandoned several hundred years ago. Many tourists explore them each year; however, nearby there is a cave that is known only to a few people — a cave apparently carved by the original inhabitants of the area. Professional archaeologists have dated it as pre-Hittite. We were determined to locate and document the cave.

We found it with no trouble, but climbing to it was another matter. It is carved into the face of a sheer rock cliff. We climbed up the steep slopes to the base of the cliff easily. J. B. did not hesitate — he climbed up the vertical face like an experienced rock climber. I didn't follow since it is a very small cave. (At least that was my excuse.) Roger later joined J. B.; however, J. B. took many flash pictures inside the cave, the first ever taken, to my knowledge.

The entrance to the cave is a square hole, probably three feet square. Inside are two small rooms, and in one of them there are the remains of what appears to be a sarcophagus, or coffin, carved out of the mountain stone. The walls of the rooms and the sides of the coffin are extremely smooth; someone spent a lot of time carving this thing.

Ancient cave near Dogubeyazit. Both cave and carvings were carved by Pre-Hittite civilizations.

A stairway, apparently to several lower rooms, has been silted up, and is impassable. We did not have the time or tools to dig, but someone certainly should.

Surrounding the entrance to the cave, the carvers had carved a scene, and, by studying this scene, archaeologists have determined the civilization responsible for it. The carving shows two robed figures, one on each side of the entrance, each wearing a turban and carrying a staff. Between them, above the entrance, is a portion of some four-legged animal, probably a cow, goat, or sheep. The head of this animal, and most likely another figure, are eroded beyond recognition. The scene depicted is some sort of sacrifice and has been designated by knowledgable scholars as pre-Hittite.

The Hittites, if you recall, were a major nation at the time of Abraham. Abraham lived not too long after the Flood, so if this cave is pre-Hittite, then very likely it was carved by the descendants of Noah soon after the Flood.

Before leaving the area, we toured the ruins of the nearby castle. It's fun to run through the different buildings and rooms,

Ancient fortress - as seen from Pre-Hittite cave.

imagining their history and functions. There appeared to be a throne room, a mosque, a minaret, sleeping quarters (with space for a sizable harem), and an open courtyard.

That evening in Igdir a busload of Swiss mountain climbers stayed at our hotel. They were on a tour and planned to climb Ararat that week. We talked to their Turkish guide, a professional mountain climber from Istanbul. He stated that it is impossible for Americans to climb the mountain, that no permission would be given, but that he had been hired by a man named Cummings to search for Noah's Ark. Cummings, a friend of the President of Turkey, had obtained permission to climb and would be in Igdir soon. We did not tell him of our intentions or experiences. I anxiously awaited a reunion with my good friend Eryl Cummings.

July 31 - Monday

Roger and J. B. planned to solicit a second permit, while Bill, Skip, and I tried to hike to Karadag. Roger dropped us off at the construction site that we had blundered into the day before and planned to meet us later. We started walking around 9 a.m. We needed to cross a ridge before we could begin searching. Bill and Skip convinced me that it would be easier to walk around this foothill than to go over it. So we followed "eshek" (donkey) trails in the wrong direction for miles.

Rain fell intermittently throughout the day. Twice we had to huddle up under rocks for shelter. And once the fields got wet, walking was even more difficult. I cannot overemphasize the magnitude of Ararat. It looks small but keeps going forever. At 2 p.m. we still hadn't reached the top of the ridge where we could begin searching with field glasses. Bill and Skip wanted to turn back, but I wanted to see what was over the ridge, so we quickened our pace. Near the top of the ridge, I instructed them to wait and rest while I ran to the top. It was still 300 to 400 feet to the top and they were tired and anxious to leave. But the view from the top was discouraging. There was only another ridge.

From that vantage point, however, I could see clearly the way down. It was more direct and the climb was easy. It only took us two hours to walk back to our rendezvous point and it took us six hours to walk in.

Roger and J. B. had had a profitable day. They had visited the Sergeant that we had met in Erzerum. He had introduced them to the Commander in charge of the entire district. The Commander was very friendly and helpful, and, although he could not issue a permit for the Ahora district, he wrote a letter of introduction and recommendation to the Commander who could. We were all very thankful for this letter and realized once again that God had His hand on our expedition and was continuing to lead.

August 1 - Tuesday

When the offices opened in Base No. 8, we were there. Skip and I remained outside so we would not be recognized. J. B. and Roger talked through an interpreter to the Commander and acquired the permit — and a most wonderful permit it was. Unlimited in time, it restricted us only from the peak of Greater Ararat and all of Little Ararat. This was far beyond our dreams.

Muhtar, in Ahora, was very upset and hurt when we showed him the permit. I think he was planning to blackmail or steal or something.

We were in high gear now and excitement was in the air as we made plans for the hike the next day. Roger, J. B., and I would retrace the route the three had taken the week before. We hoped to make it to the top of the gorge and look down onto the object that Roger and I had seen from below. We also hoped to get a better look at the object Skip and J. B. and Bill had seen on their way back from their disastrous hike. We made arrangements with Nusret, a young man whom we had come to trust, to rent a horse to carry our heavy packs up the mountain.

Spirits were high that evening. We had great expectations for the coming week.

August 2 - Wednesday

We had almost entirely packed the previous night, leaving only one tent standing. So Bill and Skip slept in the bus until we woke up at midnight. Then they went to sleep in the tent and we prepared our gear. Finally, Nusret showed up with his horse. The horse carried all three packs, about 200 pounds, while we walked carrying only rucksacks. The horse kept sitting down and falling

53

down under the weight, but we made good progress throughout the morning.

At 10,500 feet elevation, the horse could go no farther. There was no more grass, just mountains of loose rock. So we said goodbye to Nusret (or Freddie, as we called him), shouldered the packs, and continued walking for about two hours. We located the same spot at which the other group of three had camped previously and we camped there. The other group, carrying their packs the entire way, had taken two days to reach this area, while we made it, with help from the horse, before noon on the first day. The 10-hour climb had not tired us out too much. We were in good shape to continue climbing the next day.

The finger glacier on which we were camped didn't look too long or steep. It was flanked on both sides by mounds of loose

Finger glacier from below. Elevation of top, 14,000'; elevation of bottom, 11,000'; slope at bottom, 30°; width of glacier in center, 400'.

rock, very hard to walk on or over. The group before had carved out a flat area to sleep on but now it was filled with rock. We did not know why.

As we read the Scriptures and prayed that evening, I was overcome by the feeling that at the top of the finger glacier we would see Noah's Ark. I just knew that tomorrow would be a special day and related this to the others. Our spirits were high and we felt the nearness of the Holy Spirit.

Chapter Six

A Day to Remember

August 3 - Thursday

Several times throughout the night I woke up in anticipation of the day to come. The feeling remained during breakfast and morning devotions. As we packed our gear, I again shared this excitement with J. B. and Roger. I was sure that August 3rd was going to be a special day.

As we, talked, I heard a noise up above us on the slope. I looked up just in time to see a rock bigger than my head hurtling through the air right at my head, traveling at great speed and only a few feet away. I ducked instantly and it whistled by just 6 inches away. We stood in stunned silence for a few seconds, until we saw dozens of such rocks speeding toward us from above. We left our packs and ran up the side slopes, off the glacier and onto the loose rock. We watched as these rocks bounced all around where we had been standing, expecting to see our equipment demolished at any second, but the shower was over within a minute and no damage had been done. We sat there for a while, thanking God for His protection and asking for His guidance.

Once our courage returned, we stepped back onto the glacier. Again the rocks came. But we were watching for them and were up the slope before they reached us; however, one stray rock narrowly missed J. B. The situation was indeed grim. We knew the only way up that slope with such heavy packs was on the glacier. We also knew that to stay on the glacier was very dangerous. Furthermore, we knew that the Lord had called us to do a job, sent us halfway around the world, and protected us all the way. So we claimed that protection, preferring the danger to turning back.

Many more times throughout the day we were subjected to similar rock slides. The slope steepened, causing poor footing and slowing our progress, as well as making it more difficult to avoid the slides.

At one point the side slope which had provided us some protection dwindled down to very little. I raced up this small slope once to avoid a slide, but the rocks continued up the slope right at me. I ripped off my pack and threw it down and began dodging, running, jumping, falling, and praying, trying to avoid the rocks. On these loose rock slopes one finds it very hard to be nimble footed, especially when wearing metal crampons. But the Lord was in complete control, and I escaped without a scratch, even though many large rocks passed within inches.

The rocks vary in size, from walnut size to Volkswagon size, but at such dizzying speeds, even the small ones could kill. We had developed a keen awareness of rock slides weeks ago in the Ahora Gorge, but these slides were vastly different. They make very little noise on the snow, but fall with such force that they shake the earth. The speeds probably reach 100 m.p.h. Their bounces are unpredictable, and it is hard to get out of their way. As they fall, they fly through the air, sometimes for hundred of feet, spinning like a wheel and whistling like shrapnel. Each rock is like a buzz saw and would destroy anything in its path, but we felt we were in the Lord's will and continued climbing the slope.

We had camped at the bottom of the glacier. From that vantage point, we surmised that our climb would be rather easy and short. Much to our dismay we found that we had been deceived. We had camped on a slope of about 30°, digging out a place for the tent. I suppose we subconsciously had used this slope as a reference plane, causing the upper reaches of the glacier to appear easy to climb, but it was not easy. Most of the distance we fought with a 45° slope. Up near the top the slope exceeds 60°, and is

Telephoto of finger glacier.

almost impossible to stand on, especially with such heavy packs.

In the early afternoon, snow began to fall, slowly at first, but increasing rapidly. Out of the gloom we clearly heard a whistle, a store-bought whistle. Since we were over 13,000 feet elevation, this was *impossible* — but we *heard* it again! Over the ridge, maybe 200 feet away, was a man, hollering to us in Turkish. We couldn't tell what he was saying nor could we imagine why he was there. The only thing we knew was that he had a gun, and it was pointed at us. When we identified ourselves as Americans, stating that we only knew a little Turkish, he slowed down and I could understand him; but what he said, as near as I could tell, was not pleasant. He ordered us to get off the mountain or he would shoot, it was as simple as that. I told him, shouting above the rising storm, that we had official permission, that the local army knew of our whereabouts, and would miss us if we didn't return. I told him that we were just climbing up the mountain for our own reasons, that we were friends of Turkish people, not spies. This didn't seem to make any difference to him. He even raised his gun as if to fire several times. Once I tried to walk over to him but he waved me back, so, we again had to rely totally on the Lord for protection. We told the Lord that if He wanted us up the slope that He would have to take care of this man. Then we stood up, put our packs on our backs, and walked away, up the slope. We never saw him again.

The snow was falling harder. It was sliding down the slope, covering our knees at all times. The wind was blowing hard and it was difficult to see. We stopped under a big rock, providing us a little shelter from the wind and since the time was 1:00, we broke out our trail food. As we ate, Roger dropped his sunglasses, and they fell down a hole at his feet. As he reached his hand down after them, he discovered that the hole went forever. Come to find out, we were standing on a thin ice covering over a large crevasse where the rock and ice separated. Needless to say, we moved.

Since the snow was coming down in such torrents, and we were on the steepest part of the glacier, we decided to rope up, cross the finger glacier to the other side, and continue our ascent on the rocky-side slope. The rocks were almost completely covered with freshly fallen snow and were much more stable than before.

We got the feeling that we were right in the middle of a war. It seemed that Satan was doing his best to destroy us, and God was protecting. Remember, I had felt that this day we would find the Ark. Satan must have felt the same thing and was desperately trying to stop us in time. He must also realize the tremendous impact such a discovery would have on the world. But we were filled with a real peace, knowing that no matter how tough the going got, the Lord was protecting and leading, and nothing could happen unless the Lord allowed it to happen. We were in His will and on His mission and whatever happened we knew would be according to His purpose. How wonderful it is to be a Christian and know that you are right where God wants you.

The weather got worse. The temperature dropped, the wind blew harder, and the snow got thicker. We were on a slope of about 45° only 100 feet below the ridge or shoulder of the mountain where we had planned to make camp, when thunder clapped all around us and lightning struck nearby. Lightning began striking all around. Every large rock in the area was struck repeatedly.

This was the first time I was ever in a storm — I mean *in* a storm. We were actually in the clouds. Lightning was not striking in bolts, it was just collecting at one place or another. The thunder was deafening, all around us. Static electricity was evident everywhere. Our ice axes and crampons were singing, our hair was standing on end, even J. B.'s beard and my moustache were sticking straight out. We could feel the electricity build up until it collected on some nearby rock.

In our training we had been taught to avoid electrical storms if at all possible, but if ever caught in one to try and stay away from large rocks. The storm had come up quickly, and we were surrounded by big rocks and just below the ridge of huge rocks. Our only hope of safety was to continue upwards over the ridge of rocks and onto the relatively flat glacier, staying close enough to big rocks so that we ourselves would not be struck directly.

Although we were in a most dangerous situation, I felt that we would not be struck. I knew that Satan was again trying to stop us, and that God was allowing the storm, but protecting us, and that if we kept our faith in Him, with His help we would overcome the situation.

The wind and snow kept increasing as we neared the top. At one point, J. B. sat down beneath a large rock to rest and gain some relief from the blinding snow. I had seen lightning strike this rock several times and returned to warn him, but as all three of us stood or sat on this big rock, lightning struck it again, sending unbelievable jolts of electricity through us.

J. B. was frozen to the rock by his back. His arms and legs and head were extended out into the air. He was in no pain at that time even though he could feel electricity surging through his body. From that vantage point, however, he could see Roger and me thrown off the rock. The force of the lightning seemed to suspend us in the air and then dropped us far down the slope. At this point, J. B. succeeded in forcing one of his legs to the ground, completing the electrical circuit, and the force somersaulted him down the mountain, following Roger and me.

I had been standing on the rock (now known as "Zap Rock") when the lightning struck. Once again I had been thanking the Lord for protecting us, feeling that we would not be harmed. When the bolt struck, my whole body went numb, and I could

"Zap Rock".

not see or move, but never lost consciousness. I fell over back-
wards, still wearing my heavy pack. I expected an impact but it
never came; it seemed like I was floating very slowly for several
seconds. I was gently lain on the snow by unseen hands and began
sliding down the steep slope. I knew I must stop, and, for an instant, my eyes and arms would not function. When they did, I
spied and grabbed a rock in the snow, stopping my slide.

For a few seconds I lay there, not moving, aware only of in-
tense pain. I reasoned that since the pain was so great, that I
had received the full force of the bolt, and that the other two
were unaffected. I tried to roll over and sit up, but to my horror,
found that both legs were paralyzed. There was no sensation of
touch or life in them, just burning, searing pain.

I called to my friends for help, thinking they were unharmed,
but the only answer was another call for help. Looking back uphill, I saw J. B. sitting up in the snow, about ten feet away,
obviously also in great pain, with one leg twisted underneath him.
He also was paralyzed and thought the one leg was broken.

We remained there for some minutes, crying out to God for
relief from the pain and deliverance from the horrible death that

surely was to be ours. Suddenly I missed Roger, and called to him, frantically looking around for him. J. B. spotted him, much farther down the mountain, lying face down in the snow, one side of his head covered with blood. We were unable to go to him, but prayed for him and called to him from above. Finally, he stood up, looked around and walked up to us. His face was at least as white as the snow, and his eyes were filled with confusion and fear. He did not come all the way to J. B. and me but, from a few feet away, bombarded us with questions. "Where are we? What are we doing here? Why don't we go sit under that big rock and get out of this snow?" J. B. patiently tried to explain to him that we were on Mt. Ararat, looking for Noah's Ark, and had just been struck by lightning under that big rock.

Roger was in shock and experiencing total amnesia. He didn't know who he was, who we were, he didn't know anything; furthermore, he didn't even like us. He wondered who these two nuts were sitting in the snow, freezing to death, when they could gain some shelter from the storm up among the rocks. J. B. convinced him to go get our ice axes, but that was the only thing he would do to help.

Slope below "Zap Rock".

62

So J. B. and I, unable to help ourselves, had to rely totally upon God. We reasoned that Roger would slip into deep shock soon and would need medical attention. J. B. thought his leg was broken, and both of us were paralyzed, unable to move. We discussed the possible descent of the mountain, but ruled it out as impossible.

Our situation was, in short, critical. Unless we were able to get to some shelter, we would die within a few hours, freezing to death in the storm. And so, not being able to see any way to alter the situation, I prepared to die.

That's a weird feeling, rationally knowing that you are about to die. I never once doubted my salvation and did not fear death. In fact, I felt real peace, knowing that soon I was to be with my Saviour in Heaven. I had always envisioned meeting Jesus face to face as a rather exciting experience, but I now felt no excitement, just comfort. In fact, I wanted to get on with it — to die now, rather than slowly over a period of hours.

As I sat there, contemplating the horrible death in store, the Holy Spirit began to interject some of His thoughts into my mind. First, I was reminded of the hundreds of thousands of Christians who have suffered and died while following the Lord's leading, and how they considered it a privilege to suffer for Him. Then I was reminded of the marvelous way in which our group had been led in the past months and particularly the past weeks in Turkey. I was reminded of the miraculous acquisition of our VW minibus, of the Christian friends who had helped us, of the granting of the impossible permits, of all the many deadend streets down which we had wandered, only to find an open door at the end. I was reminded of the Christians back home who were praying for our safety and success. I was reminded of the job we had been called to do and its implications, importance, and urgency.

And then the conclusion! No, I wasn't going to die. God still had a purpose, a job for us to accomplish. He wasn't going to let us die up in that frozen wasteland. Somehow, He was going to remedy the situation, heal and strengthen our bodies, and allow us to continue the search for the Ark.

I was reminded of two passages of Scripture, James 5:15, which states that "the prayer of faith shall save him that is sick," and I John 5:14,15, stating that "this is the confidence which we have in Him, that if we ask anything according to His will He listens to us. And since we know that He listens to us in whatever we ask, we also know that we have the request made of Him."

These thoughts were all whirling around in my head at dizzying speeds. I knew that I wasn't going to die. I knew that I was going to be healed. I knew that this was according to God's will. And since I knew these things, the realization came suddenly that I also had faith that these things would come to pass. And if I had that faith, then I could pray the prayer of faith. And so, with my heart pounding wildly, I prayed that prayer of faith, knowing that the Lord heard me and knowing that He would answer my request and heal my body.

Before the Holy Spirit had directed my thinking, I had prayed for relief from the pain and for healing. But it was a prayer of desperation, not of faith. This time I expected a miracle. I tried to move my legs — no response. Or did that toe move? Frantically I began massaging my legs and could feel the firmness return. There was no sensation of touch in them, just a burning numbness. Before when I had felt them, they resembled a balloon filled with water, shapeless and pliable. But now they were hard. I continued to massage, covering them with snow to ease the burning sensation. Their strength gradually returned, but still no feeling. Within thirty minutes my knees would bend! Within an hour, I could stand!

Using an ice axe as a cane, I hobbled over to J. B. and massaged his legs. He had been unable to reach his ankle and still thought it was broken. We determined that it was not broken, but both legs felt like jelly. He was quite calm and relaxed and felt that Roger needed attention more than he.

Roger was sitting on a nearby rock, obviously cold and still in shock. He didn't even have the sense to put on heavier clothing. So I retrieved his pack and re-dressed him — nylon pants, down parka, wind parka, and pancho. As I was tying his pancho up around his chin, a look of recognition crossed his face, and his memory began to return. When he asked why I was dressing him, I knew he was going to be all right. He did not fully recover for several hours, but in the meantime was able to heat some water for a hot drink. In doing so, we lost all of the coffee, cocoa, tea, soup, all hot drink material. It slid down the hill, along with some valuable equipment.

J. B. had been massaging and flexing his legs all this time. His right leg had recuperated somewhat, and he could move it. Roger and I helped him over to a rock where he was able to don warmer clothing and find shelter from the storm.

Finally, I began to dress myself. My legs were weak and shaky. I had walked up and down the slope, gathering gear, until exhausted; but together we huddled under the rock to gain shelter from the storm, drink a hot drink to ward off hyperthermia, and prayed to gain victory over the situation.

Earlier, the Holy Spirit had given me the knowledge that it was in the Lord's will for us to be healed and to survive the ordeal. Now we were partially healed and growing stronger each minute, but we still faced a cruel blizzard with little chance of survival. Lightning was still flashing everywhere, snow was still coming down in buckets, and gale winds were blowing. We knew we were going to survive, but that it wouldn't be easy.

We, as Christians, are expected to have faith, large amounts of it, in fact; but we must never expect our faith to be sufficient. Frequently the Lord requires hard work and then rewards our faith by blessing our efforts. Such was the case on the mountain. The only possible area of safety was on top of the ridge away from the big rocks. We needed a flat place to pitch the tent and gain shelter from the storm, so as soon as the lightning intensity lessened, Roger and I began searching for a way to the top.

The wind was blowing the snow so hard we could not see more that 10 feet maximum, but we located a path between several huge rocks and climbed it. It was nearly vertical and footing was treacherous. Once we reached the top, however, we found the weather worse. We were right on the edge of the Parrot Glacier, and the wind velocity doubled, but we picked out a flat place to camp and returned to J. B.

J. B. had been massaging and exercising his legs. His right leg had regained its strength, but no response from his left. He still could not move, so Roger and I climbed the slope with our packs and made plans to anchor the rope to a rock and assist J. B. in his ascent. I was nearly exhausted after this second climb. My legs were shaking like rubber, so I rested in the snow for several minutes. We descended once again to J. B., and much to our surprise found him standing up waiting for us. His legs still had no feeling, but their strength had returned enough to allow him to stand, so Roger carried his pack and, with little assistance from me, J. B. climbed that vertical slope on two numb weak legs!

Within minutes of the time we reached the top, the storm broke. I guess the Lord figured that we had had enough. The snow and wind stopped, and the clouds disappeared just as suddenly as they had appeared. In complete comfort and peace we were able to pitch our tent and eat a hot supper. In fact, that evening before the sun went down, it was rather warm and pleasant.

Throughout the day, you remember, I had felt that this would be the day we would find the Ark. This feeling was strengthened by the fact that Satan was so determined to stop us. It's not hard to imagine what I was doing and thinking as we pitched the tent and set up camp. As soon as time permitted, I wandered off to the edge of the Ahora Gorge, positive that the Ark was in full view. I did not approach any dangerous cliffs, but with binoculars searched in all directions from a safe vantage point. Much to my disappointment, I did not see the Ark, but the view of the gorge from above was magnificent. The freshly fallen snow covered everything above elevation 9,000 feet, including, I suspected, the Ark. So we had to settle for a comfortable place to sleep, hot food, and our lives that night. We were satisfied and gave thanks to God. Very few people have ever camped that high on Ararat, but I'm sure no one else has had such a wonderful time of prayer and singing as we had that evening.

Chapter Seven
Majesty of the Mountain

August 4 - Friday

It is very difficult to sleep at such high altitudes. We anticipated this and took sleeping pills before retiring, but J. B. and I still did not sleep well. We were up early, noting that all the water was frozen, even inside the tent. So after melting snow for cooking and drinking, we ate a good breakfast.

J. B. had no feeling in his left leg and was still quite limited. His right leg and both of mine were functional but weak, so activities of the day were unusually light. In the morning we all hiked around the top edge of the gorge, looking over and taking many pictures. We searched for the object that J. B., Skip, and Bill had seen. With J. B.'s direction, Roger and I hiked all over the area but didn't see anything and concluded that it must have been a rock formation that they had seen from a great distance. We returned to the site of the previous day's lightning experience and marveled how the Lord had spared our lives on that steep slope the day before. We nicknamed the rock on which we had been standing when struck by lightning "Zap Rock" (I can't remember why).

The Cehenum Dere is a huge semi-circular section cut out of the west side of the Ahora Gorge. It is rimmed on top by a sheer ice cliff, 300 vertical feet thick in places. This cliff is the edge of

Object hunting from top of Cehenum Dere.

Funnel-shaped Cehenum Dere.

68

the permanent ice cap, and as the glacier moves, the cliff breaks off and falls down into the Cehenum Dere. All of the rock that is exposed in this area is weak and crumbly. Whenever we were forced to walk on it, we roped up and anchored to the biggest rock we could find. No one could venture into the lower reaches of the Cehenum Dere and expect to come out. There is nothing to walk on, nothing to hang from, and nowhere to go but down. The edges are vertical, just below the ice cap, but began sloping towards the gorge farther down. The entire area appears funnel shaped and drains down into two major chutes or gullies. These funnel slopes are hidden from view below, and we had no prior knowledge of this condition.

The crumbly rock continually breaks off and falls, along with pieces of the ice cliff. Every minute, rocks were falling down the funnel into the two major chutes below. The fall is about 2000 feet and the rocks reach great speeds. Anything in the path of

Beautiful view of ice cap.

these rock slides would be totally destroyed within days. However, our object, which we wanted to observe from above, was in one of those chutes. We could not see it, due to the ruggedness of the area, but surmised that there was not enough room for an ark 450 feet long, nor was there enough snow and ice to keep it frozen year around, nor could it have survived 5000 years of constant avalanche activity, so we turned our attention elsewhere.

J. B. remained in camp to rest and recuperate, while Roger and I walked along the terminal moraine of the huge glacial ice cap to the west of camp. I knew from Eryl Cummings' research that Hardwick Knight had found a field of timbers somewhere in the area, but the snow storm of the day before had covered everything, ruining any chance of relocating that spot.

We walked westward until a large finger glacier, one of the main ones of the Parrot Glacier, prevented us from continuing. We couldn't cross the glacier without being roped up and couldn't rope up without three people, so we returned to camp just as the afternoon grew colder. We kept a wary eye upon the approaching clouds, but they never reached us or caused any trouble.

We all needed sleep, so we took enough sleeping pills to kill a horse and went to bed, but again I had a hard time falling asleep.

August 5 - Saturday

J. B. still had no feeling in his leg but was able to walk. So the three of us roped up and walked onto the glacier, carrying food and water for the day, but no heavy gear. We wound our way through heavily crevassed areas, observing and looking for likely areas as we went. We saw several places where the glacier appeared to level off or become stationary near huge rocks, ice cliffs, or flat finger glaciers. We checked out as many as we could, but were not able to approach all. Everywhere the snow covered the ice, sometimes to great depth. Once again, I don't know what we would have found if so much snow had not fallen two days earlier.

One area was of particular interest to us. A series of four finger glaciers ran downhill for 2000 feet and appeared to level out and stop. In such a place the Ark could have been preserved. As we debated on whether or not to descend to them, a storm began coming up the mountainside and engulfed the area in question. Since we were several hours from camp and had no desire to

70

tangle with another storm out in the open, we turned tail and walked back to camp, arriving there nearly exhausted.

A glacier, when it moves, moves with tremendous force. Nothing can stand in its way, particularly a wooden structure. In order for the Ark to have been preserved for 5000 years, it would have to have been in a stationary ice pack, not exposed to the tremendous sheer forces generated by a moving glacier. The wooden Ark also would have to have been frozen almost constantly throughout history. Reports say that the wood is very hard, impregnated with a resinous substance, but not petrified, still wood in a frozen state. Other reports indicate that wood has been seen at the bottom of a crevasse. This is not at all likely because a crevasse is the result of a moving glacier. A crevassed area can be compared to rapids in a river, wherever the going gets rough, irregularities form; however, in a stationary ice pack, melting and settling can occur in a small area, usually due to under-the-surface water flow, and cause a trench to open up. This would not be a crevasse, but could be called one. Nevertheless, as we sat around

The edge of the permanent ice cap and our trail.

Rock cliff (covered by ice), at 15,000' elevation.

camp that evening, we all agreed that these areas must be searched in detail and made plans to send a group up from that side of the mountain to search the promising areas.

Before the sun set, Roger and I again roped up and walked to the edge of the Cehenum Dere. We took many more pictures of the area and spent a great deal of time searching with binoculars. We were satisfied once again that nothing of any size could be there and that nothing could withstand the avalanche activity.

We were all subject to headaches and loss of appetite at this altitude. J. B., still not fully recovered from the lightning bolt experience, was hit hardest of all by these other troubles.

Chapter Eight
Down to Earth

August 6 - Sunday

Descending the finger glacier was almost as hard as ascending, and more tiring. There is a method of climbing known as rest step which allows the climber to ascend for long periods of time while conserving his energy. But this step cannot be employed on down hill slopes. The muscles and bones of the climber's legs must absorb all weight and shock of each step.

We descended the finger glacier adjacent to the one on which we had come up in hopes that it might be more stable. We did not rope up or walk together for fear of causing rock slides. One by one we would descend approximately one hundred yards, then take cover while the others took their turns. The ice glacier was covered only by a few inches of wet snow, which would collect on our crampons (spikes) decreasing the traction on the hard ice. Several times we slipped and fell, partially due to the top-heavy packs we were carrying; but soon we were down off the ice and, after crossing a boulder field, stepped onto the grassy lower slopes of the mountain. We ate a hurried lunch near a crystal clear spring at elevation 11,000 feet and began the long, long hike back to camp.

We ran into a few rock-throwing kids, several teeth-baring dogs, and a cross-eyed bull on the way down, but otherwise the

Descent finger glacier.

descent was uneventful. My legs were very weak and shaky, and I was forced to stop frequently. The constant strain of the downhill steps had taken the strength and stamina remaining from the day of the lightning. J. B. was in much the same boat. Roger, however, was still fresh and ready to go. We gave him the heaviest pack, hoping to slow him down, but it didn't work; he was still faster and stronger than anyone else.

We finally reached Ahora in the late afternoon. When we stopped at the spring to refresh ourselves before crossing the river to camp, we noticed that our tent had been moved. It was pitched near two other tents and two other cars were nearby. We arrived at the camp at precisely the same time as a group with horses and mules arrived from the opposite side. I recognized Mr. Cummings and his party returning from a climb to the other side of the Ahora gorge.

Mr. Cummings was in the company of many people, three of whom had doctor's degrees in various fields (including Dr. L. Hewitt, longtime Ararat explorer), two jandarm, one interpreter, two young men, Mrs. Cummings, Mrs. Hewitt, and many local guides. Many of the townspeople had come out to watch. With all of these people (including us) in such a small area, there was quite a bit of confusion. So many had just returned from the upper slopes and wanted to take care of themselves and their gear, those who remained in camp wanted to hear of the results of the trip, the guides wanted to be paid, the local people wanted to have their pictures taken, and everyone was hungry and wanted supper. Someone a few days before had taken a shot at our minibus and everyone had to look at and feel the bullet hole. If Ringling Bros., Barnum and Bailey ever go to Turkey, they could not put on a better three-ring performance. Good times were had by all.

Bill and Skip told us of their week. The night after we had left, they had heard someone outside the tent, trying to break into the minibus. They ran out and scared him off, but he tried again the next night. This time Bill shot his flare gun into the air, lighting up the area. The thief must have been thoroughly frightened,

"Freddie" and his friends.

because ten or so minutes later he began shooting from the cover of the rocks. He shot twice, both times missing the tent, but one bullet hit the minibus just above the gas tank. Cummings and his party arrived the next day. When they heard of the incident, they invited Bill and Skip to join their camp, and take advantage of their protection.

After supper, Mr. Cummings invited me to accompany him to town. The two ladies had decided to wait in the hotel in Dogubeyazit until the men were finished for the year. Several of the others had only planned to spend a few days on the mountain and needed to return to America. On the way to town we had a wonderful time singing hymns and sharing experiences.

Once all the problems were solved in town and additional supplies purchased, Cummings and I headed back to Ahora. We were both very tired but managed to keep each other awake talking about what had been accomplished and future plans. I told him of my "object", but we could not decide if it was the same as in his picture. We agreed to discuss it more when the picture and maps were available.

August 7 - Monday

Roger, J. B., and I were so tired from the previous day's descent that we needed a day of rest. So we watched while Mr. Cummings and Dr. Hewitt rode off in search of Karadag, or Korhan, as it is now called.

We planned to send Roger, Bill, and Skip up to search the finger glaciers observed from above. J. B. and I would drive them to the end of the road over on that side of the mountain in the morning. We would attempt to visit Korhan and would rendezvous with them in five days.

Since Roger had been such a valuable climber and leader the previous week, and since he was familiar with the area in question, I decided to put him in charge. Neither Skip nor Bill was particularly happy about this but they were willing to accept it.

August 8 - Tuesday

We had planned to leave Ahora before dawn and drive to the new area in order to give the climbers an early start, but we got a late start and did not arrive in Igdir until 9:00 a.m., still

76

an hour's drive to the "end of the road." So all agreed that we should spend the night in Igdir and leave early in the morning.

J. B. and Bill had been faithfully checking the post office for any news from home, and on this day, their diligence paid off. J. B. received one letter, and Bill six.

Checking the food supply, it was discovered that there would be only three day's supply left after this five-day trip was over. I had sent word to Jack not to drive out from Adona, because we had no place or time to meet him; so, in order to continue the explorations, we would have to drive back to Adona and re-supply.

Everyone was cross and out-of-sorts and much in need of a day of total relaxation and rest. J. B.'s foot still bothered him quite a bit, so on Dr. Hewitt's orders, Bill injected him with some Vitamin B_1. Both Roger and I also received shots, just in case some damage of which we were unaware had been done by the lightning. My legs were still quite sore from the strain of the climb, but that had nothing to do with the lightning.

Rugged formations southwest of Mt. Ararat.

During the afternoon, Skip became acquainted with a young Turk, an engineer who had been educated in America. He spoke very good English, and during supper he told us an interesting tale. While traveling through the area a few days earlier, the local army had apprehended and detained him. He had been mistaken for a Communist agitator who was instrumental in causing a riot in Western Turkey. He had just been released from jail after word was received that the criminal in question had been killed earlier in the week. Our friend had, however, shared his cell with many hardened criminals, several from the region we planned to investigate. He said that the entire side of the mountain was inhabited by fugitives, living outside the law and hiding from it. He advised us not to enter that area.

While we were talking, Mr. Cummings approached our table. He also stressed the fact that the people of the western side of the mountain were lawless, and that he had been robbed at gunpoint there several years earlier. He insisted that we not go there without guides and protection. He emphatically stated that our previous permits were not valid on that portion of Ararat.

Later in the evening, we reflected on these two warnings. We all felt that we should continue our search in that area, but that it must be done legally and safely. It seemed that God had brought the Turkish engineer and Mr. Cummings to us to warn us of a hazardous situation, so, late at night, J. B. and I entered the appropriate army headquarters and applied to the sergeant in charge for a permit to visit that area. After a few cups of tea, he gave us a permit. Once again, we had cause to praise God for His leading and provision.

August 9 - Wednesday

We reached the end of the road shortly after daybreak. After breakfast and a devotional, Roger, Bill, and Skip took off. Roger was irritable and worried about his responsibility.

J. B. and I drove to Dogubeyazit for breakfast, fixed the car, and bought some food from the local market. We had decided to conserve our package food as much as possible, in case it was needed for another climb.

We visited the hot springs at Diyadin for two reasons; first, so that we might get pictures of the impressive geology in that

Earthquake fault zone near hot springs.

area and also pictures of the hot springs themselves (this geology supports very well the theory of a worldwide flood in recent times); second, both J. B. and I were still feeling the effects of our bout with Mother Nature and Ararat and desired the soothing effect provided by mineral water.

The hot springs are a tourist attraction of sorts, but only Turks were there. In the morning, the women are allowed to bathe, and the men in the afternoon, so we photographed until noon and then went in. The water is not in a natural pool, but piped into a concrete pool inside an uncovered building. The water is very hot, hotter than any other mineral water I have ever felt. After several enjoyable hours of hot water and hot sun, we left, both a healthy pink.

When we passed through Dogubeyazit on the way back, we stopped for a coke, and to our surprise found Mrs. Cummings and Mrs. Hewitt in the hotel there. They were waiting until their husbands were finished with their work.

Back in Igdir, we tried to line up some horses for a trip to Korhan. The local civilian veterinarian introduced us to a farmer who was willing to guide us for a large sum of money. We didn't trust him and declined the offer, deciding instead to return to Ahora, hire Freddie (our Turkish friend) and his horses, and approach Korhan from there.

My legs began to stiffen up. I purchased some heating rub from a drug store, and generously rubbed it in that night. Within a few minutes, I was running and jumping around, throwing water on my legs and screaming for help. The hot water and sunburn had made the skin sensitive, and the medicine must have been for horses. I believe this hurt more than the lightning. At the next Geneva conference I am going to suggest that this type of torture be outlawed. I gulped down four pain killers and two sleeping pills before the pain was bearable, but I still didn't sleep well that night.

Geyserite formation at hot springs.

Mt. Ararat and the Ahora Gorge.

August 10 - Thursday

After arriving in Ahora at noon, we made arrangements with Freddie. He agreed to take us and our equipment to Korhan for two days for 175 LIRA (about $12.50) a day. Cummings was preparing to spend the next six days up in the far reaches of the Ahora Gorge with his Turkish climbers.

I spent a long time trying to translate the strange words written on the back of the tube of heating rub. Neither my Turkish training, nor books, nor dictionaries solved the mystery.

Chapter Nine
Mysterious Writings From Long Ago

August 11 - Friday

Freddie arrived at 5:00 with two horses and two donkeys. One donkey carried our gear, and the other carried Freddie. I rode a healthy horse, slow, but sure-footed. J. B. rode a nag.

The trails were very narrow, but well-worn, and usually easy to see. They traversed up and down and around, over, and through some of the most rugged country I have ever seen. All of the northwestern side is lava-flow, one steep slope after another, covered with sharp broken rock. Our horses frequently balked, refusing to move. J. B.'s horse continually stumbled — it didn't appear to have much natural coordination. Even on level ground it walked funny, sometimes unable to decide which foot moved next. I usually brought up the rear and enjoyed the comical scene in front of me — Freddie chasing the two donkeys, who continually strayed from the trail, beating them and kicking them until they obeyed, and J. B., an expert horseman, trying to control his temper as his horse slipped and tripped along. I suppose if someone had been observing me, they would have received an additional laugh, for I am no horseman and my horse, who was lazy, frequently tried to take off-the-trail shortcuts, finding out too late that the terrain is almost impassable anywhere else.

The road to Ahora.

Ancient altar on lower slopes of Mt. Ararat.

83

Our saddles were the best in Ahora (says Freddie), but they weren't much — just a piece of shapeless leather with semi-adjustable stirrups. The reins on my horse had been broken many times and were tied together with string. They were so short I couldn't reach them easily, so usually I just dropped them and let the horse follow the others.

Several times J. B. and I got off and walked, because that was less painful than riding, and also because the horses refused to go certain places and we had to drag them along. It took almost five hours to get there.

We pitched our tent at the foot of Korhan and ate lunch. Freddie took one bite of our salted bacon bar and threw up. All three of us felt sick, and we suspected that a melon we had eaten earlier had spoiled. There was plenty of dry grass around but no water of any sort. We had plenty for ourselves, but the horses had none.

Mt. Ararat is a volcanic mountain. Now dormant, it has experienced several periods of activity. During one of the later periods most of the lava spilled out onto the northwestern quarter, flowed down the slopes, and covered the surrounding plains for a distance of twenty miles away from the mountain. Korhan is a mound in the middle of this lava flow. The elevation of its base is approximately 6,000 feet, while its summit is nearly 7,000 feet. Nearly a perfect cone, its sides are extremely steep and ascent is difficult. The slope farthest from the mountain is the least steep, but it is the most inaccessible.

As a stranger enters this area, he is struck by both the ruggedness and the remoteness. Present-day civilizations have left their mark. The Kurds use this area in the winter to shelter their flocks of sheep and goats and have constructed large low buildings, only 4 or 5 feet in height, to protect their livestock from the snow. Seldom does anyone enter this area during the summer. Armenians used Korhan as a burial grounds, it seems, for around the base, many ornate headstones remain, some with crosses and candlesticks, and some with writings.

We climbed up the southern face, keeping an eye out for snakes. The entire area exhibited an air of antiquity; each step seemed to send us farther and farther back in time. Every large rock appeared to have markings on it, as if it had been carved, or handled by someone. Many had small round holes in them, as if clamps

Ancient altar of Korhan.

Rock with ancient carvings, both pictorial and cunieform.

or hooks of some sort had been used to haul them up the mountain. All of the major rocks were dense, black, and heavy, incongruous with the surrounding area. We were sure that most of them had been dragged up the mountain and placed in patterns or structures by some ancient people, and now were displaced.

Several days earlier, Cummings and Hewitt had relocated the area and many of the objects mentioned in the files of Colonel Koor, formerly of the White Russian Army, but had failed to rediscover the ancient writings carved into a large stone supposedly near the summit. As we climbed, we investigated each large stone, finding many with what appeared to be the remnants of writing on them, but their surfaces were so marred and weathered we could not be sure; but near the summit, as we passed between two large rocks and entered into an area that appeared to have retained more organization than elsewhere on the mountain, we saw the writing.

It was as if the stone marked the entrance to a particular area, for the most logical path to the summit led right to it, and behind it a trail appeared with stones placed almost in a staircase pattern. It was as if someone had placed a sign over the door of an important place, a sign of welcome, or identification, or perhaps warning.

I am not surprised that the others had not found it, for the weeds had grown up and covered a good portion of it. It was situated so that the sun did not shine directly on it for much of the day, and was totally weathered in portions and covered by lichens in others.

Several crosses had been cut deeply into the rock. They caught my attention first and were apparently added in more recent times, adjacent to some very clever pictorial writing. On the far right-hand side was the cuneiform writing, wedges making up patterns and symbols — all just as Koor had recorded. It was a very gratifying experience for me, knowing that we had made a significant archeological discovery, and that in all likelihood no other outsiders had seen this carving in over sixty years; so after a word of thanks for the discovery, and a prayer for a more important discovery farther up on Mt. Ararat proper, we pressed on.

We followed the crude stairs up to the very top of the mountain and, much to our surprise, found a rather large flat area. The mountain had appeared completely conical from below, and we

Eight crosses on tomestone near altar.

were sure the peak was pointed also, but the cone is truncated at the top, causing a flat, circular area of about 100 feet in diameter.

On all sides of the peak, except the approach side, are the ruins of stone walls, perhaps four to six feet tall in places, but all in a rather bad state of repair. On the western-most side, a striking block structure dominates, balanced on the edge of a sharp drop-off and overlooking the entire area. It is approximately 30 feet in height, rounded on one end, but flat on the two sides. The side facing the center of the plateau is open, with steps leading up into it. The walls are about 12 inches thick and appear to be charred or baked on the inside. Several feet of sediment or hardened ashes cover the floor. At the foot of the stairs we noticed a bowl carved into the rock, possibly a wash-basin. The workmanship is excellent — few ruins that I have ever seen, other than the prominent and beautiful Greek and Roman ruins, have been constructed with such accuracy and care as this edifice.

I am no archeologist and did not make a detailed study and certainly did not excavate, but I can make a guess as to the original use of this structure, just as I can rule out other possible explanations. It does not appear to be a fortress or a lookout tower, simply because it was too small to contain men for long periods of time. Furthermore, it has no windows, and the additional elevation would provide no change in the sight distance of an observer. I feel that the structure was an altar, probably used for sacrificing large animals. Noah himself built an altar when he disembarked from the Ark, and the location of that altar is not specified in the Bible as high on Mt. Ararat. Perhaps — who knows?

One other possibility presents itself. Near the base of the structure, is another graveyard containing about twenty graves, suggesting that possibly the structure was used as a crematory. I have no evidence to support this theory except that the inside of the structure appears to have been burned and charred.

Carved on most of the gravestones are crosses, extremely well shaped and some very well preserved. The most prominent stone is right at the base of the block structure and is decorated by eight crosses. Mr. Cummings has seen these crosses and, after careful study, believes that they are ancient Sumerian crosses. Now the Sumerians are one of the most ancient civilizations that we know anything about. Whether or not the crosses are actually Sumerian, I do not know, but the fact that they are ancient is significant.

One other thing to consider . . . eight crosses on the tombstone below the altar, eight people on the Ark which landed on Mt. Ararat. Also, there were eight patriarchs who had died before the Flood, and some ancient traditions suggest their remains had been taken on the Ark. Coincidence? Maybe. I am not qualified to say.

The only other major object seen on the plateau is near the entrance to the area. A pool or fountain is carved into the rock and flanked on two sides by benches. The pool is about 6' by 4' and fairly well preserved.

Below the walls and surrounding the peak are open pits, perhaps 25 of them. Speculating again, I would say they have been used as altars also, either by those not privileged to use the large structure on the plateau, or by more recent civilizations who refrained from using it, but sacrificed to the same Being for the same reasons.

One of many sacrificial pits surrounding altar of Korhan.

To the southwest, we observed more ruins at the base of Korhan and descended to them. As we walked through waist-high weeds, we continually stumbled and fell over large stones and walls hidden from view. I could not even guess what treasures are buried there.

The ruins that we had observed from above are obviously the remains of a huge and well-constructed building. The inside walls are circular, but the outside walls are square. As near as I can tell, the only room is shaped similar to a three-leaf clover. The walls vary in thickness from 4 feet to 8 feet and are composed of large well-formed rectangular blocks of stone, cemented together with mortar. Once again, on the outside we discovered pictorial writing and crosses. It is obvious to me that this building was not at all functional, but was a shrine or temple built by some ancient people, commemorating something very meaningful to them. It is a shame that the destruction of the structure is so complete.

As far as I know, no professional archeologist has seen these ruins. If their worth is only a fraction of what I suspect, they

Shrine at foot of Korhan.

should be excavated fully. One day, perhaps enough interest will be stirred up in this project so that qualified scientists will seek to uncover the hidden secrets of Korhan.

*   *   *

Ten hours in the saddle is too much for a city-slicker like me. By the time we reached camp, I was too tired to stand and too sore to sit. Freddie insisted that we pay him the full price for a two-day trip even though he had forced us to return in one day (the horses had no water). After a long argument, we split the difference to get rid of him and collapsed exhausted into our sleeping bags.

Chapter Ten
The Highway Robbers

August 12 - Saturday

J. B. and I cleaned the car, our clothes, and ourselves in the morning and promptly left Ahora. J. B. was in a hurry to reach the post office in Igdir before it closed. The usual 2½ hour drive somehow took only 1½ hours, but there was no mail for us at the P. O.

We decided to check into the hotel before lunch. We were accustomed to drawing a crowd wherever we went, but we couldn't understand the reception at the hotel. The Turkish people are very friendly and curious and will surround a tourist and watch him for hours, but this crowd pressed in around us, all screaming something about guns, jail, jandarma, and Mt. Ararat. I could not tell what they were talking about but assumed they were talking about the bullet hole in the side of our car. So, before checking in, we sat down for a coke and tried to think this thing out (things go better with coke, you know). One of the young boys was talking to J. B., tugging on his sleeve and pulled him upstairs. He came down in a few minutes and dragged me up into a room, where, to my surprise, sat Bill and Skip! They told us in English the same story the people downstairs had been trying to tell, a story of guns, jail, jandarma, and robbery on Mt. Ararat!

Their story follows:

Day 1 — On the first day, they walked, carrying their heavy packs for about five hours until they met a man named Joseph, who agreed to carry their packs on his donkeys for the remainder of the day. He was extremely friendly and hospitable to them and took them to his tent for lunch. They camped at about 10,000' elevation near a little pond fed by melting snow.

Day 2 — A lady and several kids were hanging around their camp while they packed the next morning. The lady had a cow and several donkeys and offered to carry their gear. They had very little Turkish money but she agreed. At first she strapped all three packs on her cow, but three times it just moaned and fell down. Then, as she switched them onto the donkeys, a man and a boy arrived to drive them up the mountain. The boy's name was Hussain, and the man's Akita. They sang together as they walked.

Frequently, throughout the day, Skip and Bill separated themselves

Mt. Ararat from hot springs.

from the others and spent time searching the mountain with binoculars. Roger stayed with the man and boy and came to know them well. They camped near the bottom of the finger glaciers that had looked so interesting to us the week before in the early afternoon and planned their next day's climb. One old man entered the camp and snooped around, but he was their only visitor.

Late that night, they were awakened by the sound of a nearby gunshot. They heard several people moving outside and then a whole volley of shots rang out, followed by much shouting and more shots. Roger sat up and shouted back that they had permission from their friends in the jandrama to climb, but as he talked a bullet ripped through the tent, narrowly missing his head. He shouted for them to stop and crawled out. Immediately three men surrounded him, jabbing him with their gun barrels and hitting him with clubs while shining a flashlight in his face. Skip and Bill followed and received the same treatment. As they were herded out onto the rocks, all three felt that they were going to be killed. One of the men, an older man, was extremely harsh and cruel, and as he appeared to be preparing to kill them, Skip and Roger and Bill prayed for him and the others, because it was obvious that Satan was in control of their lives, and they needed Jesus Christ and His salvation desperately. One of the thieves was moved by this and restrained the older man from shooting and from any more harsh treatment. He guarded the three climbers while the older man and the third man (probably Akita, the donkey driver) cleaned out the tent, taking everything they could carry. When the thieves left, the only things they left behind were the sleeping bags, the tent, the ice axes, and the boots. These things were the only things necessary for survival and retreat back down the mountain. Nothing else could be done that night, so the three men went back to sleep.

Day 3 — On the way down, they again stopped at Joseph's tent for lunch. They arrived at the construction site (the starting point) at two in the afternoon and remained there until six, when they were given a ride to town on the workers' bus. They rented a room at the hotel, desperately in need of food and rest, but before long, the jandarm had heard of the robbery and reported the news

93

to the military outpost in whose jurisdiction the robbery had taken place. Within hours, Roger was standing in jardarm headquarters.

The Army Commander, several lawyers, and civilian officials were present, and the decision was made to return to the scene of the robbery that very night. Roger was to accompany them. So they started out in the rain and cold, up treacherous Mt. Ararat, with no provisions and only two flashlights divided among fifteen men.

They walked all night through the jagged rocks along the narrow trails, bunched together in two little clumps around the flashlights.

Day 4 — The local people, and indeed all the people of Turkey, idolize (or fear) the jandarm. Whenever they approached a village, the people would hasten to fix a meal, provide horses, sleeping quarters, etc. Often the soldiers took everything edible from a family, and the family seemed quite willing to give it. The jandarm has total power to seize anything from the people, or to punish them if they do not cooperate.

They reached the scene of the robbery at noon or so, but were unable to find anything. None of the people that they had met on the way up had any information to offer (at least they didn't offer it), and so the Commander decided to turn back.

On the way down, they encountered a man who confessed to be the brother of Akita, the donkey driver, one of the three suspects for the robbery. The brother, under duress, admitted that he had witnessed the robbery, but had not taken part in it (fat chance). He was forced to lead the entire group to Akita's tent, farther down the mountain.

As they neared Akita's village, Roger heard familiar singing, the same song Akita and the boy Hussain had sung two days earlier. Indeed, Hussain and some little girls were nearby, walking uphill after having left the very tent the brother of Akita was leading them to.

Upon entering the tent, Roger immediately recognized two of the men as having been involved in the robbery, the harsh old man and the one who had befriended them, by their voices and mannerisms. (On the night of the robbery, it had been too dark to see the faces of the thieves, especially after they had shined flashlights in the faces of the men.) Akita was not present. Roger didn't accuse the men that evening, since they planned to sleep in the tent that night. He did, however, request that the guards stand watch throughout the night.

J. B. and I checked frequently with the officers in charge at headquarters for any news concerning Roger, but communication lines were dead.

August 13 - Sunday

Early in the morning, Roger and the Commander called all the men of the village together. One by one, Roger made them shout the phrases he had heard the thieves shout, and once again he recognized the old man and the friendly one as the guilty parties. When the old man was accused, he transformed himself from a gruff, cruel Kurd to a holy man, kind and gentle. He ran in the tent, brought out a prayer rug, and began bowing to Mecca, bragging that he was too holy to commit a crime. He could not have acted any more guilty.

The five I.C.R. expedition team members.

The Commander arrested the old man and ordered his men to search the tent. They found no equipment of ours, nor did they find any guns. (This is unheard of on Ararat, guns are a status symbol among the Kurds and play an important role in their everyday life.) Akita's brother was arrested as an accomplice along with the children. The entire group descended the mountain and returned to town.

J. B. and I were waiting at the army headquarters when they drove up, about twenty people in one truck. Roger and the officers ate a good meal and questioned the suspects in the presence of Skip and Bill. Neither Skip nor Bill recognized any of the suspects, but both agreed that they did not pay close attention to either Akita, Hussain, the girls at the camp, or the thieves. The Commander agreed, however, with Roger that the Kurds that had been apprehended appeared to be guilty. He vowed to continue to search for Akita and suspected that they would find the stolen goods when they found him.

We spent a good portion of the day with the Commander, supplying him with a detailed list of the equipment stolen, mailing addresses, names, etc. After supper we met again, and Roger, Bill, and Skip signed official reports and complaint documents.

*　　*　　*

Now everyone would agree that the robbery was a most unfortunate experience. That our expedition was abruptly halted, just as we were about to enter the most promising portion of the mountain, is indeed distressing. But one of the most wonderful things about being a Christian is that the events of our lives always have a purpose, even though very often we cannot see that purpose. We can claim the promise of Romans 8:28, knowing that all things *do* work together for good to them that love God, to them that are called according to His purpose. We also know that when God makes a promise He is going to keep it, and our situation was no exception.

Throughout the three days of investigation, a deep personal friendship had been established between Roger and the Commander, a warm, open, young officer. This friendship was broadened when the Commander met the rest of us, and when we left he invited us back, promised to provide us with permits to visit the mountain, offered us the use of his men for protection, and indicated that he would aid in any way. Furthermore, he promised to make every effort to apprehend the criminals and return our equipment. Our equipment, camping, climbing, and photographic, is valued at approximately $3000.00, but this friendship and promise of future access to the mountain must be valued much more highly.

Chapter Eleven
Enough for Now

August 14 - Monday

We left the region of Ararat early, each disappointed that we had not found the Ark, but each somewhat relieved that the trip had come to a close. The constant stress, hardship, and sickness had given each of us a better understanding of God, as well as an appreciation for the blessings of home. Some internal friction had built up among us, and it is doubtful that the team could have continued to function in harmony much longer.

But we also realized that we had, with God's help, accomplished much, and the invitation to return was overwhelming.

August 15 - Tuesday

J. B., Skip, and Bill left on the plane around noon. Roger and I remained in Ankara to tie up loose ends.

August 16 - Wednesday

Roger and I met with our Christian friends at the little church and told them of our experiences. Everyone received a blessing, especially me. These Christians, from all faiths, are among the most vibrant, joyful Christians I have ever met. They live in a Muslim country, far from the conveniences most of us take for granted, such as the choice of many churches, TV, and radio services, and fellowship with others. Yet, they joyfully serve God in these adverse circumstances.

August 18 - Friday

We left Ankara but our plane was grounded in Istanbul. A small plane crashed on takeoff and we were given lodging in a swanky Tourist hotel at the expense of the airline.

August 19 - Saturday

Finally, we left Turkey, made good connections in Frankfort and New York, and flew all night.

August 20 - Sunday

We arrived in Los Angeles in the early morning, six weeks and one day after that wonderful group of Christian friends and relatives had seen us off — but there was no welcoming party, for no one knew exactly when we were coming. While waiting for someone to pick us up, I had time to relax and reflect on our trip.

There had been hardships, more frequently and more severe than we had expected. Bad food and the resulting diseases, unsanitary living quarters, long, treacherous, unpaved roads, hot weather, cold weather, people with whom we couldn't communicate — all these things had stood in our way before we even reached the mountain; and once on the mountain, we found the sinister, gun-toting Kurds, dirty water, insects, avalanches, rugged slopes, crevasses, lightning, and thieves.

But then there had been blessings, far more rich and meaningful than are experienced under normal conditions. There was the friendship of five men, drawn together in a common cause, serving and worshiping God together. There were the many Turkish friends, some of whom we had told of Jesus and they had readily listened; also, the American friends who had given us their fellowship and prayers when we needed them most. The car had been acquired in a miraculous way against impossible odds. The unavailable permits had been issued as an answer to prayer. The nearness of the Holy Spirit, while expecting death in the electrical storm, and the subsequent divine healing is something I shall never

Mt. Ararat; the birthplace of modern civilization.

forget. Simply being on Mount Ararat, realizing the significance of the mountain in human history, and knowing that Noah's Ark is somewhere nearby is in itself a rich blessing. The protection of God's children when threatened by murdering bandits . . . the list could go on and on.

And then I remembered the people here in America who had supported us, in deeds, financially, and with their prayers. I remembered how much easier it had been to bear up under the hardships, knowing that hundreds of people were praying continuously for us. I knew that the blessings heaped upon us had been the result of their prayers, as well as ours. It made me ashamed to think how often I had promised to pray for someone and hadn't. I remembered how Paul had realized the value of Christians praying for each other when he wrote in II Corinthians 1:8-11:

"I think you ought to know, dear brothers, about the hard time we went through in Turkey. We were really crushed and overwhelmed, and feared we would never live through it. We felt we were doomed to die and saw how powerless we were to help ourselves, but that was good, for then we put everything into the hands of God, who alone can save us, for He can even raise the dead. And He did help us, and saved us from a terrible death; yes, and we expect Him to do it again and again. But you must help us too by praying for us. For much thanks and praise will go to God from you who see His wonderful answers to your prayers for our safety!"

We had set out looking mainly for Noah's Ark. We had not found it — but we had accomplished many important goals, and I remembered *them*. We had climbed all over Mt. Ararat, ruling out all but a few areas of the mountain as possible areas of search. We had taken many pictures of areas no one had ever reached before. We had gained a working knowledge of the mountain. We had also completed a geologic survey begun by others. We had documented three important archeological sites in the Ararat region. We had relocated, and photographed for the first time, the Korhan inscriptions originally discovered by Col. Koor many years ago. And, most important, we had been invited back.

God has a timetable, I am sure, and it seems likely that Noah's Ark will once again play an important role. If the Ark still exists at all, it has been supernaturally preserved for these thousands of years, and if God has put forth this effort, it follows logically that He will reveal the remains when the time is exactly right, as an encouragement to believers and/or a sign to unbelievers.

Obviously, 1972 was not the year during which God's timetable demands the revealing of the Ark, but the possibilities for the coming years are exciting. It seems to me that all indicators are pointing toward the immediate future, but I don't know the timetable. I do know, however, that the Lord has opened the doors for us to return soon and continue the search.

As for this trip, I consider it a major success. We went in the Lord's will, following His leading, and for His glory. We went in prayer and with the prayers of many believers. We went so that men might come to know Jesus Christ as personal Saviour, and that the faith of Christians might be strengthened. No, we didn't find Noah's Ark, but soon, perhaps, someone will. For I am convinced, that as powerful as the Prince of this Earth may be, he does not have the power to thwart or alter the progress of God's Eternal Timetable.

Epilogue

For nearly three months following the robbery of August 10, I was satisfied that the loss of our equipment was allowed by God and was used by Him to grant permits to a following team of explorers. It was a high price to pay, but I knew that if He wanted us to return, He would open the doors and make the necessary finances available.

As we left Turkey, the Commander promised to continue the search for the thieves, and, if any of the equipment was recovered, he would mail it to me through the American Embassy; but I did not expect any major results. I may never get used to the way God operates, but He did it again. On the night before Thanksgiving when the lost equipment was the farthest thing from my mind, it was returned.

The Turkish people are generally poor. The money from the sale of the equipment would have been a fortune to anyone there. But yet it was returned.

The results of this may not be immediately obvious. First of all, it seems that the Lord intends for us to reuse this equipment on Ararat, and not be forced to re-purchase similar gear. It also appears likely that the bandits (part of a large ring of thieves living on Ararat) have been apprehended and that the most promising portion of the mountain is safe for exploration. But most of all, the friendship established with the Commander has lasted, and the permission to climb is still available. The door remains open.

Appendix A
The Center of the Earth

The earth's surface is approximately 70% covered with water, which part is thus uninhabitable by man. The 30% of the earth occupied by land surfaces is not in one single land mass, but is stretched out in an odd-shaped assortment of continents and islands, all of which are either inhabited or potentially habitable by man.

It is significant that ancient secular historians, as well as modern archeological researchers, all agree that the development of civilization began somewhere in the so-called "Bible lands" — not in Europe or America or China or South Africa, but rather somewhere in the region where Asia and Europe and Africa join together, most likely in the Tigris-Euphrates region. The ancient natation, of animal domestication, of agriculture, and of most other antiquity, were all centered around this area.

Similarly, the beginnings of written communication, of transportation, of animal domestication, of agriculture, and of most other basic ingredients of structured human economics, focus on this region. All of this is so well known and universally accepted that we need not attempt to document it here.

At first, one might be tempted to offer these facts in support of the divine inspiration of the Bible, since the Bible does indicate that civilizations existed before the Flood and that, therefore, men carried with them aspects of that common civilized knowledge as they gradually spread around the world from Mount Ararat and the city of Babel. These facts, do of course, support the general historical accuracy of the Bible, but the historical fact that civilization began in this region does not in itself demonstrate that the writer of Genesis required divine revelation in order to report that fact correctly. He may simply have been a good historian. The rise of civilization in that region might be attributed to favorable physical and climatological conditions rather than to the Genesis story that Noah's Ark landed in the vicinity.

However, there may be a more subtle correlation between the Bible and geography than this, one which cannot be explained in terms of natural physical factors such as climate and soil fertility.

The argument might go like this: since God intended for man to "fill the earth" after the Flood (Genesis 9:1), and since the Ark "rested upon the mountains of Ararat" the very day that God restrained the Flood from further destruction (Genesis 8:1-4, compared with Genesis 7:11), wouldn't it be reasonable to think that God had arranged for the "port of disembarkation" to be located somewhere near the geographical center of the land which man was commanded to fill?

This may not be a necessary inference, but it does seem the most appropriate thing for God to do, since He was at this time acting completely in grace toward Noah and his sons. At any rate, it seems to be worth investigating as a hypothesis.

As a matter of fact, the location of the earth's geographical center should be a matter of some value entirely apart from any theological considerations. In addition to its purely academic and aesthetic interest, there could be innumerable future applications of this information. If ever there is to be a world administration, or a world communications center, or a world center of education or transportation, or commerce, or almost any organized activity of mankind as a whole, the most efficient location for such systems would logically be near the geographical center of the world's inhabited lands.

Other things being equal, the cost of operating such systems would be minimized and the ease of utilizing such systems would be maximized if their hubs were located reasonably near the center of all the sub-systems around the world that would have to be keyed into them. The location of the center of the earth is thus important not only esthetically and theologically, but also scientifically and economically.

Until the present time, however, such information could not have been acquired at all. In the first place, the geography of the earth's land areas would have to be mapped with reasonable accuracy, and this was not accomplished until modern times.

However, the structure of the continents and islands is so intricately complex that there is no feasible way of calculating their center exclusive of the use of a high-speed digital computer.

The process is this. Divide up all of the land area into small unit areas. The "center" that we are looking for, then, is that particular unit area for which the average distance between it and all other unit areas is a minimum.

To accomplish this calculation requires a knowledge of spherical trigonometry, geodesy, calculus, and computer science. In addition, there must be available accurate data on the earth's land and water areas, arranged in a grid network tied to latitude and longitude. With these factors present, the computation then becomes quite feasible.

Results

This particular research investigation was first proposed by Andrew J. Woods, M.S., a physicist with Gulf Energy and Environmental Sciences in San Diego. The project was sponsored by the Institute for Creation Research to the extent of providing funds for computer time rental and for publication of the resulting Technical Monograph.[1] Mr. Woods performed all the analyses and programming on his own time. His results are summarized in the form of a project report, included as Part II of the Monograph. The theory behind the analysis, the computer results, and his conclusions are all given in that section.

The most significant conclusion, of course, is that the geographical center of the earth is indeed located in the so-called "Bible lands," as the Biblical and theological considerations discussed earlier would infer.

---

1 Technical Monograph No. 3, Institute for Creation Research, San Diego, 1973.

This fact is significant statistically. If we consider the Bible lands to be bounded roughly by Memphis (the capital of ancient Egypt) on the south and west (latitude 30°, longitude 31°), and Ararat on the north and east (latitude 39°, longitude 44°), this will include Babylon (latitude 33°, longitude 44°) and Jerusalem (latitude 32°, longitude 35°), as well as practically all the cities in which the events narrated in the Old Testament took place. The land area contained in this quadrangle (between latitudes 30° and 39°, and longitudes 31° and 45°), is approximately 440,000 square miles. The total land area of the earth's surface is approximately 197,000,000 square miles, 450 times greater.

Therefore, the probability that the earth's center would happen to fall in these Bible lands is only one chance out of 450. This is highly significant, from a statistical point of view, even more so in light of the Biblical inferences to this effect, and is strong evidence of divine planning. The events could just as well have taken place, so far as chance is concerned, in any one of 449 other land areas of equal size elsewhere, land areas *not* containing the earth's geographical hub.

The *exact* center of the earth, in so far as Mr. Woods' calculations could determine, was found to be near Ankara, the present capital of Turkey, at latitude 39° and longitude 34°, on the same latitude as Mount Ararat and essentially the same longitude as Jerusalem.

Theologically speaking, it might have seemed more appropriate for this exact center to have turned out to be in Jerusalem, or else at Mount Ararat or possibly Babel. Of these three, it is essentially equidistant, about 550 miles, from Ararat and Jerusalem.

However, since there is no explicit statement in the Bible requiring the earth's center to be precisely at Ararat or Babel or Jerusalem, all of the implications of Scripture in this regard are well satisfied if the center is somewhere in these Bible lands.

Interestingly, the earth's center at Ankara, along with Jerusalem, Ararat, and Babylon, form almost a perfect square. As far as the needs of a potential center of world activities are concerned, these also would be met by a site anywhere in this region. Other factors besides that of precise centrality would, of course, have to be considered in the choice of such a location.

The calculations made by Woods indicate, in fact, that the average distance to all the world's land areas varies only slightly for any central site in all this general region. The average distance from the Ankara region is 4597 miles, whereas the average distance from the Jerusalem area is 4612 miles, and from the Ararat region is 4617 miles, a difference of only 15 miles and 20 miles, respectively, or about 1/3%. In terms of practical applications, the difference is negligible.

By way of contrast, the location of the earth's "anti-center" — that is, the point with the *greatest* average distance to all the earth's land areas — was found to be in the South Pacific, at a point of latitude –45° and longitude –150°. This point is east of the southern tip of New Zealand and west of the southern tip of South America, far from land of any kind. This would be the *worst* place to locate any kind of world activity center! The average distance to the land areas of the earth from this point was found to be 7813 miles.

Appendix B
Brief History of the
Evidence for Noah's Ark

The undertaking of a dangerous and costly expedition to Mount Ararat in search of Noah's Ark naturally raises questions of a pragmatic nature. Did such an Ark ever really exist at all? What good would it do to find it even if it did? Why pick Mount Ararat as the place to look? Even if it were there originally, how do we know it has been preserved all these years?

The first question is the only one that can be answered with complete confidence. The Ark *did* exist! This fact is confirmed not only by the record of the book of Genesis (chapters 6-9) but also by the Apostle Peter (I Peter 3:20), the writer of Hebrews (chapter 11:7), and by Jesus Christ Himself (Matthew 24:38; Luke 17:27). Mohammed also refers to the Ark (Koran, Sura XI, 40), as do a great many other religious writings of the world's ancient nations and tribes.

The second question can also be answered positively, though not so directly. The Ark is described in the Bible as a gigantic barge, approximately 450 feet long, 75 feet wide, and 45 feet high. It was built to house representatives of all the land animals, as well as Noah and his family, and to preserve them through the worldwide cataclysm of the Deluge. According to the record in Genesis, the flood waters rose higher than all the mountains and the Ark floated freely for five months. When the waters began to recede, the Ark rested on "the mountains of Ararat," but it was another 2½ months before the tops of the adjacent mountains could be seen and an entire year before the occupants could leave the Ark and descend the mountain.

Many modern intellectuals are highly skeptical of this story. They do not believe in a universal flood, nor in Noah, nor in the Ark, nor in much of anything connected with the Bible. The confirmed discovery of Noah's Ark would surely go a long way toward re-establishing popular confidence in the authority and reliability of the Bible. It would open the door for witnessing to many people who may before have been indifferent.

It would certainly be the greatest archeological discovery ever made. Other human artifacts are almost invariably found in the superficial deposits of post-Flood cultures and civilizations. The Ark may well constitute the one remaining man-made link to the antedeluvian world. If the Deluge story is true, the pre-Flood civilizations were either destroyed so completely or buried so deeply that any remains of them are unlikely ever to be found. There are occasional reports of man-made structures or implements found deep in the coal strata or other geological formations, but these are difficult to document and easily ignored by the scholars. A huge sea-going vessel found high on a great mountain could hardly be ignored!

Suppose the Ark *were* found and definitely confirmed, high up in the permanent ice cover of Mount Ararat, as the reports allege. What could the scholars possibly say to try to explain it away?

Certainly no one would ever have attempted to construct such a structure in such a location! Neither could or would anyone have towed it up there from somewhere else. The mountain is a volcano, subject to intermittent eruptions and earthquakes even in recent times, and it would be clearly providential for it to be there at all.

The only conceivable way by which the Ark could have acquired such a location is by having been floated into place from its construction site. And the only way *that* could have happened is by means of a flood of such magnitude as necessarily to be a universal flood.

A person would have to be wonderfully naive concerning the behavior of water to believe that the Ark could have been deposited near the summit of Mount Ararat by a local flood!

Thus, the presence of Noah's Ark in this position would demonstrate openly and conclusively that the flood of Noah was really and truly a worldwide flood after all, despite the dogmatic denials of four generations of "historical geologists."

Furthermore, there is one more conclusion. A worldwide flood could not be a "tranquil" flood! It would literally devastate the globe. Any geologist who can believe in a worldwide flood that would leave no observable changes on the earth's surface, when he already is committed to believing that the sedimentary fossil deposits which "identify" his "geologic ages" were formed by a great host of "local floods") can believe that winds don't blow and fires don't burn.

A system of historical geology which is based on uniformitarianism necessarily denies any kind of worldwide cataclysm; therefore, proof of a worldwide cataclysm would demand a complete restructuring of the present orthodoxy of the geological establishment. The discovery of Noah's Ark would immediately render the current premises of historical geology totally obsolescent. The geological ages, purportedly five billion years in duration, would have to be converted into diluvian stages totalling approximately one year!

Such a development would apply the final death-blow to the already fragile philosophy of Darwinian evolution. The supposed evolutionary succession of fossils in the geological ages is the only historical evidence for evolution. If the geological ages are imaginary, then their evolutionary implications are likewise imaginary.

The Ark, therefore, could well provide the final, climactic testimony to this present evil world that God is Creator and His Word is true. Evolution and all its progeny (communism, fascism, racism, animalism, etc.) are exposed as utterly and openly false. The age-long Satanic opposition to God's purpose in creation could no longer be masqueraded as "science," but would have to surface as overt Satanism. It is hardly surprising that such tremendous difficulties are encountered by those who try to find the Ark!

As far as the location is concerned, this also has been a problem. Although the Bible clearly says the Ark rested on "the mountains of Ararat," other claims have been numerous, each "flood legend" having its own suggestion.

Furthermore, there exists a difference of opinion among scholars as to whether the two "mountains of Ararat" now known by the name ("Big Ararat," 17,000 feet high, and "Little Ararat," 13,000 feet high) are the same as those mentioned in the Bible. This name has been applied to an entire region, as well as to a kingdom, in ancient times. Furthermore, other names than Ararat have been applied to the mountain known by that name today.

Nevertheless, even allowing for these uncertainties, it does seem probable that the present Mount Ararat is really the mountain where the Ark landed. The ancient inhabitants of the region, the Armenians, have for at least three thousand years attributed Noah's landing to this mountain. The same is true of the almost equally ancient Persians, as well as the Kurds, who still inhabit the region near the mountain's base.

Mohammed, in the Koran, says the Ark rested on Al-Judi, a mountain believed by some to be far to the south of Ararat; however, many Muslim scholars agree that Al-Judi is merely the Arabic name for the same Mount Ararat.

This question has occupied the attention of a number of scholars, whose opinions and evidence are ably summarized in Violet Cummings' book *Noah's Ark: Fact or Fable?* The reader is directed to that volume if he desires full documentation of the case for Mount Ararat.

But there is also another reason, less "scientific" but no less cogent. Mount Ararat is the highest mountain in the region, and one of the highest in the world. It is surely one of the most majestic peaks one could imagine, rising in solitary grandeur from the plains below. When the factors of divine providence are considered, this is clearly the most *appropriate* place for God to terminate Noah's world-spanning voyage. According to Scripture, after the Ark rested, it still took 2½ more months of recession of the waters before the tops of the other mountains could be seen. Ararat uniquely fits.

Furthermore, for the Ark to be preserved, as tradition says it has and faith believes it has, it would have to be at an elevation sufficiently high for ice to encase it most of the time. Again, only Ararat meets the condition in that region.

Finally, the name itself is providential. The Bible identifies the

111

Ark with Ararat and, regardless of the history of the region, this is the mountain with that name now!

While such evidences may be less than compelling to the intellectual, they seem adequate to the eye of faith. We believe they justify an intensive search of Mount Ararat for the actual remains of the great vessel.

The numerous rumors and reported sightings of the Ark likewise focus on Mount Ararat. Though no one of these is conclusive in itself, the large number of them certainly suggests there is something to it. An effect must have an adequate cause.

Listed below are a number of the most significant reports. For details, see Mrs. Cummings' book *Noah's Ark: Fact or Fable?* These reports are listed chronologically.

(1) Ancient historians such as Josephus, of the Jews, and Berosus, of the Babylonians, mention in their writings that the Ark was still in existence at the time of their writing.

(2) Medieval historians and travelers, such as Marco Polo, likewise point out that, according to the Armenians, the Ark was still at that time preserved in the mountain where it had grounded.

(3) The early 19th century was a time of conflict between the uniformitarians and catastrophists. Much of the opposition to the growing evolutionary sentiment was based on the history of the great Flood. In about 1856, a team of three skeptical scientists journeyed to Ararat for the specific purpose of demonstrating once and for all there was no Ark there; however, their Armenian guides led them up to the mountain directly to the Ark. In their anger, they threatened death to the guides if they ever told anyone about it.

Many years later, one of the guides, by then known as Jeremiah the Pilgrim, related the story, shortly before he died, to friends in America. At about the same time, one of the atheist scientists also told the story in a deathbed confession, which was reported in many of the papers of the time, but soon forgotten.

(4) Sir James Bryce a noted British scholar and traveler of the mid-nineteenth century, conducted extensive library research on Ararat and was convinced the Ark was preserved there. Finally, he himself ascended to the summit of the mountain in 1876 and found, at the 13,000 ft. level, a large piece of hand-tooled wood, which he believed was from the Ark.

112

(5) In 1883, according to a series of newspaper articles, a team of Turkish commissioners, while investigating avalanche conditions on Mount Ararat, unexpectedly came upon the Ark, projecting out of the melting ice at the end of an unusually warm summer. They were actually able to enter a portion of the Ark, but the press reports maintained only an attitude of scoffing at the account.

(6) Archdeacon John Joseph Nouri, born in Baghdad, was the recognized leader of the Nestorian Christians of his day, a small but ancient sect whose modern remnants are found primarily in Persia and Kurdistan. They are related also to the considerably larger groups of Mar Thoma Christians in India and similar sects in other Asiatic countries. Nouri apparently was esteemed in all these and widely traveled and educated. According to his claims, he had made three attempts to scale Mount Ararat, which was not far from his homeland, to find the Ark. On the third try, he succeeded, entering the Ark and confirming that its appearance and measurements corresponded to the Biblical account. This was in 1887. Six years later, he addressed the World Parliament of Religions in Chicago concerning his discoveries, but apparently his story made little impression on the liberal churchmen assembled there.

(7) In 1902, and again in 1904, an Armenian boy and his uncle climbed to the Ark and the boy actually entered it. In his day, many of the Armenian Christians of the region, descendants of the people who had lived there since the earliest days, evidently knew how to reach the Ark and had seen it. However, the Armenian massacres destroyed many of them and scattered the rest. The Armenians who still live in the area are almost all now in Russia and thus inaccessible to westerners. Years later, as a very old man in America (he died in 1972), he described the Ark to interested researchers, and it is from his description that the sketches given in Mrs. Cummings' book were drawn.

(8) One of the most widely-circulated Ark stories was that of its discovery by a Russian aviator flying over the mountain in 1915, during World War I. The news of his discovery reached the Czar, who dispatched a large expedition to the site. The soldiers were actually able to locate and explore the boat, but before they could report back to the Capital, the Russian revolution of 1917

had taken place. The report disappeared, and the soldiers were scattered. Some of them eventually reached America, and various relatives and friends have confirmed to Eryl Cummings and others that they had told them about seeing the Ark.

(9) At about the time of the Russian sighting, five Turkish soldiers, crossing Mount Ararat, accidentally encountered the Ark; however, they did not report their story until 30 years later, when they offered to guide an American expedition to the site. The expedition did not materialize, however, and their services were never sought until after they all had died.

(10) An explorer and radio commentator, Carveth Wells, made an attempt to reach Ararat through Russia in 1933. He was unable to cross the border into Turkey; however, he did visit an ancient monastery nearby at Echmiadzin. The monks there strongly believed the Ark was still preserved on the mountain and showed a large plank to Wells which they maintained had been brought down from the Ark.

(11) About the same time as Wells' trip, a New Zealand archeologist, Hardwicke Knight, attempted to reach Ahora, on the north side of the mountain, by circling around from the south, near the snow line on the mountain. In the process, he came across what appeared to be a framework of heavy timbers, just exposed above the melting ice field. He did not realize until much later that these timbers could well have been a displaced portion of the structure of Noah's Ark.

(12) During World War II, there appear to have been several aerial sightings of the Ark. One of these was reported in 1943 in the U.S. Army paper *Stars and Stripes,* in a Tunisia theater edition. Although many ex-servicemen have confirmed seeing this story, it has so far been impossible to locate the exact paper to ascertain the names of the flyers.

(13) Also during World War II, a group of Russian flyers on at least two occasions took photographs from the air which showed the Ark protruding out of the ice. These were reproduced in a Russian wire-photo that appeared in various American papers.

(14) A Kurdish farmer by the name of Reshit reported in late 1948 that he had found the Ark and that other peasants had also climbed up the northern slopes to view it. However later expeditions

114

have always been unable to contact Reshit or the others who had seen it.

(15) An oil geologist, George Greene, in 1953 took a number of photographs of the Ark from a helicopter. After returning to the United States, Greene showed his photographs to many people, but was unable to raise financial backing for a ground-based expedition. Finally, he left for South America, where he died. Although no one knows where the pictures are now, many people testify that they saw them, and that they clearly show the Ark protruding from the melting ice-field on the edge of a precipice.

(16) A French contractor, Fernand Navarra, acting on information from Armenian friends, ascended Mount Ararat in 1952 in search of the Ark, and again in 1953 and 1955. Finally he found, deep in a crevasse in a large ice-field, a large wooden timber, apparently hand-tooled. Deeper in the ice, both from the crevasse and from the field above, he saw a dark mass which he is convinced constitutes the remains of the lower portion of the structure of Noah's Ark. In 1969, the SEARCH team, guided by Navarra, returned to the same site and found additional pieces of wood. The wood apparently is several thousand years old (though the radiocarbon dates were somewhat contradictory), extremely hard and impregnated with some sort of resinous material.

(17) Numerous expeditions have been conducted in the past 25 years, especially by the Archaeological Research Foundation and its successor organization, SEARCH, as well as by Eryl Cummings and by John Libi. Various others have tried also, and a great number of still other groups have applied unsuccessfully for governmental permission to search the mountain. So far as concrete published results are concerned, however, all of these except Navarra have failed. Unconfirmed rumors exist, however, of a quasi-official expedition from the U. S. government that *did succeed* in finding the Ark several years ago, bringing back extensive photographs and artifacts to document it. For reasons unknown, these have supposedly all been sealed up in government vaults, and attempts to obtain confirmation have been futile.

Most of the foregoing narratives are given in much more detailed and documented form in Violet Cummings' book *Noah's Ark: Fact or Fable?*, published in 1972. There have also been a number of other reported sightings of the Ark, but those listed above are, so far at least, apparently the most significant and trustworthy.

One would think that, with so many reports and so many attempts, the Ark would have been fully confirmed and revealed to the world long ago. Though no one or two of the reports would be convincing in themselves, the great number of them — involving many individuals and circumstances, yet all focusing on the same area of the mountain — are bound to indicate there is real substance to the belief that the Ark is still there.

Evidently, however, there are tremendous obstacles to its full and final confirmation — physical problems, political complications, financial requirements, and, perhaps most of all, demonic opposition to such a vitally significant testimony to the truth of God's Word.

If God has preserved it to this day, despite all the destructive forces of nature to which it has been subjected for four thousand years — as evidence indicates He has — then it has undoubtedly been for a specific purpose. That purpose almost certainly would be that of one final worldwide testimony to an unbelieving world just before His second coming. He will, therefore, reveal it in His own perfect time.

In order to make the greatest impact, however, the discovery would have to be announced after the world has been prepared to recognize its significance. Perhaps this is God's purpose in the long series of unsuccessful, but increasingly publicized expeditions. Also, the significant revival of interest in scientific creation that is attracting international attention today in both the popular press and the scientific journals will provide an ideal background against which to announce the discovery when it finally takes place.

Evolutionary and uniformitarian philosophy will stand openly exposed before the world as utterly false. It was by the "building of the Ark" that Noah "condemned the world" of skepticism and wickedness in his day (Hebrews 11:7). "As it was in the days of Noah, so shall it be in the days of the Son of Man" (Luke 17:26). Perhaps once again that same Ark will emerge from its age-long resting-place to condemn a similar world of scoffers and rebels today, issuing one last call to flee from the wrath to come, finding eternal refuge in that greater and more perfect Ark of salvation, the Lord Jesus Christ.

Other Books of Interest